Attributes of God

Philosophy of Religion Study Guide

Clare Jarmy

First published in 2014

by PushMe Press

Mid Somerset House, Southover, Wells, Somerset BA5 1UH

www.pushmepress.com

© 2014 Inducit Learning Ltd

British Library Cataloguing in Publication Data
A catalogue record for this book is available from the British Library

ISBN: 978-1-909618-52-7 (pbk)
ISBN: 978-1-909618-53-4 (ebk)
ISBN: 978-1-78484-000-6 (hbk)
ISBN: 978-1-78484-001-3 (pdf)

Typeset in Frutiger by booksellerate.com
Printed by Lightning Source

A rich and engaging community assisted by the best teachers in Philosophy

philosophy.pushmepress.com

Students and teachers explore Philosophy of Religion through handouts, film clips, presentations, case studies, extracts, games and academic articles.

Pitched just right, and so much more than a textbook, here is a place to engage with critical reflection whatever your level. Marked student essays are also posted.

'The unexamined life is not worth living' Socrates

Contents

Introduction

The attributes of God are a foundation for a study of the Philosophy of Religion. Consider other important topics dealt with in the subject, such as:

- How the world got here

- Whether the world is designed

- Where good comes from

- How evil is explained

- Whether we can speak of God

- Whether there are miracles

- Whether God reveals Himself in the world

- Whether there is life after death

Any discussion of these subjects rests on an idea of what God is. If God created the universe, then He must be outside space and time as we know it, and must have extraordinary power. If He is a designing God, He must have great intelligence. If He is the explanation for goodness, He must Himself be good.

Many of the questions asked in the Philosophy of Religion already **PRESUPPOSE** certain attributes that God has. Take the example of religious language. We would not ask the question of whether we can talk about God unless we already believed Him to be, in some way, outside the system, or at least very different from things we normally talk about.

Or take the question of how the world got here. The fact that God is seen to be one of the possible answers to this question shows what we already believe about God's attributes: that He is powerful; that He could be the creator.

So the kinds of questions asked in the Philosophy of Religion can presuppose, and assume, certain attributes that God is said to have. It is therefore extremely important to talk about the attributes of God themselves, and enquire whether they are cogent. If the idea of God makes no sense, then that threatens many of the other questions in the Philosophy of Religion.

ATTRIBUTES OF WHOM?

Despite the fact that a lot of topics in the Philosophy of Religion presuppose certain things about God's nature, the concept of God is far from straightforward, and there are many reasons for this.

The first reason is that the idea of God has many **INFLUENCES**, from Jewish religion and Greek Philosophy (amongst others), which are amalgamated - and this amalgamation becomes a tradition. The second reason the concept is complex is because **THEOLOGY DEVELOPS**. The idea of what or who God is, is something that has developed over centuries. The third reason is that the idea of God has a **PHILOSOPHICAL** role, as well as a role within **THE PRACTICE OF RELIGION**; God might be conceived differently in the Philosophy of Religion to how He might be conceived by those who practise the faith (although of course this could be seen as a false distinction, as there are many philosophers of religion who also practise a religion).

In the Christian tradition, two terms have emerged to label different conceptions of God:

- The **GOD OF THE BIBLE** (or the God of sacred scripture)

- The **GOD OF CLASSICAL THEISM** (or the God of the philosophers)

The God of the Bible is the God depicted in scripture, and is often associated with the God that is worshipped in churches, rather than the God that is studied in universities. The God of the Bible is not a concept of God that bears meticulous scrutiny by philosophers, but is a God who reveals Himself in the pages of the Bible.

The God of classical theism, on the other hand, is a conception of God that represents not simply the scripture, but the intellectual tradition of a particular faith. This conception of God has not only scriptural influences, but also philosophical ones. Philosophers in this tradition have carefully worked through apparent contradictions and difficulties in the attributes of God, in order to make them coherent. This is a highly technical understanding of God, understood by scholars, but not studied by the average churchgoer.

Just to complicate matters further, these two ways of envisaging God are not completely distinct. One of the main influences for the idea of God in classical theism is of course scripture. Also, many of the theologians and philosophers who think and write about God are part of, even at the centre of the Church. There has, perhaps, been a tendency in the Philosophy of Religion to emphasise too little the fact that these two understandings of God's attributes are both connected by tradition as well as being distinct.

HOW ARE THE ATTRIBUTES OF GOD SEEN DIFFERENTLY IN THE TWO VIEWS?

So, two different traditions have emerged, with perhaps a different understanding of the Nature of God. Let us look at how this might impact on specific beliefs about God's nature.

God's power

THE GOD OF CLASSICAL THEISM

The God of classical theism is generally held to be omnipotent, which is the idea of an all-powerful God. An interesting area for discussion is the implications of the claim that God is omnipotent - can He, for example, create a square circle? We will discuss the implications of omnipotence in Chapter 4.

THE GOD OF SACRED SCRIPTURE

The Bible does not talk of God as omnipotent, but talks a lot of His great power, as well as demonstrating it in His actions. The Bible implies, perhaps, an almighty rather than omnipotent God. On this view, God could be the most powerful being that exists, rather than an entirely powerful being.

God's relationship with time

THE GOD OF CLASSICAL THEISM

The God of classical theism is generally seen to be in some way outside of time. This has important implications for the idea of God acting in time, ie at specific times. This is discussed in the last chapter.

THE GOD OF SACRED SCRIPTURE

In the Bible, God is said to be everlasting, but it is not clear if He is ever said to be outside of time. He brings things about at certain times, so it could be argued that the God of sacred scripture is everlasting, but inside time. Having said this, there is no logical problem with the biblical God being outside time.

God's goodness

THE GOD OF CLASSICAL THEISM

The God of classical theism is seen to be wholly good. Aquinas, in way four of his "five ways" argues that a wholly good being is needed to fully explain all lesser good in the world. Elsewhere, he argues that we can know something of God's goodness, because we recognise goodness in the world, and by analogy know the goodness of its creator.

THE GOD OF SACRED SCRIPTURE

Like the tradition of the God of classical theism, God's goodness is clearly portrayed in the Bible. What is meant by God's goodness is an interesting question, however. In Chapter 3, we will examine how God's goodness is portrayed in the Bible, and whether we can infer from scripture that God is indeed good.

God's knowledge of our future decisions

THE GOD OF CLASSICAL THEISM

The God of classical theism is understood as being omniscient, meaning that He knows everything. Now, if He knows everything, it follows that He knows the future. Much philosophical ink has been spilt over the question of whether God can know what you are going to do, without that compromising your freedom. We will examine Boethius's and Aquinas's response to this in Chapter 5.

THE GOD OF SACRED SCRIPTURE

The Bible portrays God as knowing what we will do, and even "determining our steps". God's omniscience has more biblical support than the idea of His omnipotence, for example.

God's creative power

THE GOD OF CLASSICAL THEISM

The God of classical theism, because of the influence of Aristotle's thinking, is believed to be creator ex nihilo (out of nothing).

THE GOD OF SACRED SCRIPTURE

There is a question of whether the Bible depicts God as creating ex nihilo or not. In the second chapter, we will examine all the evidence carefully.

God's acting in the world

THE GOD OF CLASSICAL THEISM

The God of classical theism is (again, because of Aristotle's influence) held to be immutable, which means He never changes. This has obvious implications for whether He can do anything, because acting seems to imply that you have to change in some way.

THE GOD OF SACRED SCRIPTURE

The Bible seems to claim that God is both unchanging, but also undergoes things happening to him, such as finding things out, or being disappointed by a person's action. The Bible therefore seems to give a somewhat confused or at least confusing account of whether God is unchanging.

KEY TERMS

GOD OF CLASSICAL THEISM - God as discussed in philosophical discourse.

GOD OF SACRED SCRIPTURE - God as presented in the Bible.

FURTHER READING

- **DAVIES B** - An Introduction to The Philosophy of Religion, OUP 2004, Ch. 1

- **VARDY, P & ARLISS J** - The Thinker's Guide to God, John Hunt Publishing, 2004 Chs. 2&3

A history of the idea of God

KEY TERMS

95 THESES - Document written by Martin Luther condemning many of the doctrines and practices of the Roman Catholic Church.

ECCLESIOLOGIES - Different theological views and practices.

DOCUMENTARY HYPOTHESIS - The view that the Pentateuch has four different sources.

LATIN DOCTORS OF THE CHURCH - Early Church Fathers who played a key role in establishing doctrine.

HERESY - A view that departs from Orthodox teaching.

MONOLATRISM - Worship of one God: does not exclude believing there to be many Gods.

NATURAL THEOLOGY - The idea that you can use reason and the world around us as a basis on which to draw conclusions about the divine.

REFORMATION - The split away from the Church in Rome that started with Luther and people like him challenging papal authority.

SCHOLASTICISM - The movement in medieval philosophy most associated with Aquinas, where Ancient Greek ideas, particularly those of Aristotle, become synthesised with contemporary thinking.

Because the idea of God has influences, and theology develops, it is helpful to know a bit about how that development happened. Having said this, writing a brief and clear history of the idea of God is a very difficult task. We are dealing with documentary evidence that is, in some cases, thousands of years old and hence getting an accurate picture can be tricky. Scholarly opinion is divided on a number of important issues, so what we will try to do here is to give an overview that will help us to understand how ideas of God's attributes develop.

THE GOD OF THE OLD TESTAMENT

Let us turn first to the Old Testament. The Old Testament is of course not originally a Christian document at all, but is made of Jewish scripture. It is comprised of 39 books, the first five of which are known as the Pentateuch, or as the Jewish Torah. These books, Genesis, Exodus, Leviticus, Numbers and Deuteronomy, contain within them many of the Old Testament stories with which people are most familiar.

According to tradition these books were composed by Moses; conservative scholars still believe this to be the case. However, evidence for Moses' authorship is lacking. Although parts of these five books report to have been written by Moses, there is nothing in the text that claims that he authored the whole Torah. Moreover, he refers to himself in the third person. Why refer to himself as "Moses", rather than "I"? Perhaps the biggest reason for not believing Moses was the author of the Pentateuch though is that they report Moses' death; it would be quite some feat for Moses to have written about that!

An established alternative view was proposed by **WELLHAUSEN** in the 19th C, and is known as the Documentary Hypothesis (DH). This view claims that the Pentateuch has four sources composed separately, each of which has a slightly different emphasis and understanding of God.

The four sources are known by the letters: **J**, **E**, **P** and **D**.

- **J** - Stands for Jahweh, which is the name this source gives to God. The Jahwist source has an idea of God that is very directly involved with His creation: this God, for example, talks to people directly, and says he will directly act on behalf of His people. This is the God that creates Adam and Eve in the Garden of Eden.

- **E** - Stands for Elohim, the name this source gives to God. Elohim is taken to be a more generic word for any deity, unlike Jahweh, which is a more personal name for God. This is reflected in the Elohist depiction of God. This God is one that stands back from creation. He does not speak to people, or act directly on their behalf. Instead, He uses intermediaries like angels, to talk to and act for humanity. In the case of the calling of Moses, God speaks to Moses in a burning bush.

- **P** - Stands for Priest, and is a source that is concerned with priestly concerns, such as sacrifice, religious law and ritual.

- **D** - Stands for Deuteronomy. The focus for this source is the relationship between God and humanity. The term often used for God in this source is "The Lord **OUR** God", which suggests an interaction between the people and their God.

So the idea of God in the Old Testament is complex. There are a number of names given to God, each of which has a different emphasis. There are also conflicting ideas emerging about whether God interacts with creation or not.

More than this, there is also a question about whether in the Old Testament the God of Israel is the only god. Judaism today is a very clearly monotheistic religion, but there is evidence in the Old Testament that they might not have believed that their God was the only god.

In the Old Testament, the existence of other tribes' gods is not denied. Yahweh is the God of Israel; He is their God, but this does not mean that He has to be the only God. This idea, of worshipping one God, but not denying the existence of other gods, is called **MONOLATRISM**, which literally means "worship of one God".

Many think that initially, the God of Israel is conceived of as one amongst many other tribes' gods. He was their God, and they worshipped Him, but other gods existed and were worshipped by other tribes. In Exodus 20:3, the commandment given is that "You shall have no other gods before me"; perhaps this implies there are other gods.

Then perhaps they believed that their God was a more powerful God than the other Gods. We see this in Psalm 86:8: "Among the gods there is none like you, Lord; no deeds can compare with yours."

This seems to imply that there are many gods, but theirs is the powerful one.

Finally, the belief gradually developed that their God was not simply one God amongst other Gods, but was the God; the one and only. This might be illustrated in Isaiah 52:10, which says "All the ends of the earth will see the salvation of our God." This is a God for all nations, not just for the Jewish people. In addition, in Deuteronomy 4:35, we hear that "The Lord is God; besides him there is no other." So this view goes, Judaism does not start out as a monotheistic religion, but develops into one.

This hypothesis is not universally accepted and it could equally be argued that the emphasis on having "no other gods" in the Ten Commandments highlights the monotheistic outlook, rather than undermines it. Moreover, the creation in Genesis 1 seems to suggest that God made the world, the seas, light, dark, the dry ground, the sky and everything else. If the Old Testament is portraying the God of Israel as one amongst many, it seems strange that their God would be the creator of the universe.

In summary, the attributes of God in the Old Testament are far from straightforward. Different names are used for God, and if the Documentary Hypothesis is correct, different sources are making contradictory claims about His interaction with the world, or lack of it. Moreover, it is not clear from the texts of the Old Testament whether this God was conceived initially as a God amongst other gods, or the one and only God.

THE NEW TESTAMENT

The Old Testament is a story of multiple concepts of God being included, amalgamated and developed. The story of the New Testament, on the other hand, is almost the opposite of this. Jesus lived between the years of roughly 4 BCE and 29 CE, yet it took until 367 CE for the content of the Christian Bible to be decided upon.

Unlike the Jewish tradition, which has always been happy to include and grapple with different views and understandings of scripture, the early Church wanted to make sure that the Christian view was clear, and that it was specified what, precisely, they believed. The concept, for example, of the Trinity, where God is one but also three persons - the Father, Son and Holy Spirit - was one that understandably caused controversy as well as confusion. In fact, the first major division in the Church came in 1089 when the Church in the East seemed to have a different understanding of the Trinity to the Church in Rome. This was the so-called **FILIOQUE DISPUTE**, which centred around the question of whether the Holy Spirit is sent by God the Father alone (the Orthodox view) or by God the Father and the Son (the Western view).

There were many Gospels written after Jesus' death, and some of them give a pretty different understanding of who he was from the Gospel accounts we are more used to. For example, the Gospel of St Thomas is sometimes referred to as a **GNOSTIC GOSPEL**, which is to say that it has a very strong influence from Greek philosophy, specifically Platonic ideas of higher wisdom and understanding. More controversial still was the **GOSPEL OF JUDAS**, which tells the story of Jesus from Judas' perspective, correcting the idea of him as Jesus' betrayer. Some sources show Jesus as a more political figure; some show him as an almost ghostly presence. The Early Church had to decide which idea of Jesus and theology was the correct idea, and so it was not until 367CE that finally the biblical Canon was decided.

THE THEOLOGICAL TRADITION

The work interpreting Christian ideas was far from over, though. A tradition started to emerge of reasoning through the implications of Christian teachings; interpreting their significance, and building a depth of understanding in key concepts. The so-called **FOUR LATIN DOCTORS OF THE CHURCH**, Augustine, Gregory, Ambrose and Jerome (as well as many others) were instrumental in this. After this, thinkers such as Boethius, living in the 5th-6th C, continued and developed this tradition.

Although most of Plato's writings were lost to the West before the medieval period, Platonic writing was still influencing medieval thinkers, because of the influence Plato had on writers like Augustine. Christian thinking was becoming a rich tapestry of different influences.

During the time that European knights were involved in the Crusades, texts that the West knew existed, but which had been lost, were discovered in Islamic libraries, and translated for the first time into Latin. The discovery of, in particular, the works of Aristotle provided a catalyst for much important philosophical work that took place, particularly at the University of Paris in the 13th C. The movement that started as a result of this was called **SCHOLASTICISM**, and the person at the centre of this tradition was **ST THOMAS AQUINAS** (1225-1274). Aquinas synthesised Aristotle's thinking about God with the Christian tradition that came from scripture, as well as the work of earlier writers such as Augustine and Boethius. He created rational, well-argued responses to some of the key questions about the nature of God, including some of the key difficulties.

Meanwhile, in medieval Europe more generally, there were many **SECTS** of Christianity that were developing away from the central message of the Church, whom the Church pronounced **HERETICS**. It was important for the status and power of the Church, as well as the integrity of its message, that Christians stuck to one viewpoint. Groups such as the Cathars (who held the whole of creation to be evil, and spiritual escape to be the goal of life), or the Dulcinians (who wanted to overthrow the feudal system, emphasising Jesus' poverty), were usually excommunicated by the Church, which meant they were thrown out of the Church and ostracised from society. It was believed that someone who was excommunicated would go to Hell.

Someone who fell foul of the Church in this way was **MARTIN LUTHER** (1483-1546), but in his case, the result was quite different. Luther was an Augustinian monk who developed a strong awareness that not everything was how it should be in the Church. On a visit to Rome, he witnessed great impiety amongst priests, even during the Mass. People were sold indulgences by the Church to absolve them of sins they had committed; the Church was a sponge for the money of the faithful. The Church was a powerful institution indeed under Pope Leo X (of the prosperous Medici family of Florence); indeed, it had the power, through indulgences and excommunication, to save people from or condemn them to hell.

Martin Luther believed that the Church was not needed as an intermediary (middleman) between a person and their God. It should not be a person's standing with the Church that matters, but rather his standing with God Almighty. After a long time suffering with his doubts, he finally articulated them in a 95-point document that has come to be known as the **95 THESES**. Luther was excommunicated, but this did not knock him off course. Luther's thinking clearly reflected the thinking of many others at the time, which allowed his ideas to spread and become adopted by lots of people. The Lutherans, and others of similar persuasion, utilised the newly invented printing press to produce Bibles, as well as other religious pamphlets, in the language of the land (called the vernacular, for example English or German) rather than Latin, the language of the Roman Church. The Bible became central to the very personal Protestant way of worshipping, and hence ordinary people needed to be able to understand it. What started with one man standing up to the Pope caused a more general **REFORMATION** in the Church. The first division of Christians came in 1089, between the Church in Rome and the East. Now there was a new split: between those that became known as Roman Catholics, and Protestants (those who protested against the Roman Church).

Over time, two distinct approaches to God formed. The Roman Catholic view was **THE GOD OF CLASSICAL THEISM**. This view maintained that the revelation of God's nature found in scripture could be supplemented; added to, with the insights of God-given human reason. Scripture and **NATURAL THEOLOGY** could go hand in hand. The Church in Rome held that human reason was God-given, and as such, was a valid method by which to understand the nature of God. Scripture was vital to the Roman Catholic understanding of God, but was not the only source of understanding; human reason could add to it.

The Protestant approach was to focus much more on the Bible, something they had to fight so hard for everyone to be able to read. Rather than relying on the Church to pronounce how to interpret the nature of God, each person could form a personal relationship with God through prayer and scripture reading. The idea of the **GOD OF SACRED SCRIPTURE** became, therefore, much more central to Protestantism.

Today, these tendencies remain in the different denominations of Christianity, though there are now many different **ECCLESIOLOGIES** (theological views and practices), and the distinctions between different Christian approaches are now much more fine-grained. Still, within the most radical wings of Protestantism, we see a seriousness about scripture that has led some to take the Bible completely literally, as a complete picture of the world. In the most scholarly corners of Roman Catholicism, there are groups such as the Jesuits who still work to complete highly intellectual writings about the nature of God.

God the Creator

KEY TERMS

ANTHROPOMORPHIC - Person-like, a depiction of God with human qualities, perhaps those that God is not usually said to have, such as having a body, walking etc.

BARA - Hebrew word meaning "create", but a word used only of God.

EX MATERIA - Out of matter.

EX NIHILO - Out of nothing.

SCOPES TRIAL - A famous case in which a high-school teacher was prosecuted for teaching evolution.

SOCIAL DARWINISM - A view where the idea of "the survival of the fittest" is applied to people to suggest that some have more value than others because they are stronger.

TRANSCENDENT - Above and beyond; a depiction of God that is beyond this world and not contained by it.

The idea of God as a creator is an important attribute of God, recognised in both the traditions we earlier described as the God of the Bible and the God of classical theism. In the philosophical tradition (the God of classical theism), God is seen to be creator ex nihilo, out of nothing; a first cause behind the universe and an ultimate explanation of it. In the scriptural tradition (the God of the Bible), there is an interesting discussion to be had about whether God creates out of nothing (which we will discuss later), as well as fundamental questions to be asked about whether the accounts of creation should be taken literally or metaphorically.

In this chapter, we are not discussing the God of classical theism, but the God of the Bible. Therefore, when "God" is mentioned, we can take it that what is meant is God, as depicted in the Bible, rather than the idea of God within a philosophical tradition.

THE TWO GENESIS CREATION NARRATIVES

"Genesis" is the title of the book of the Bible in which we find the accounts of God's creation of the world; the first book of the Old Testament. The name "Genesis" means "origin" or "beginning"; it is from the same word from which we get "genetics" and "generation". "Genesis" is a title given to the book by translators; it is a Greek word, not a Hebrew one. In Hebrew, the title of the book is Bereshith, meaning "in the beginning", which are the words that begin the first chapter, in which the origin of the world is explained.

The account from Genesis, where God creates the world, is one of the best-known parts of the Bible, yet it is also one of the least understood. There are in fact not one but two creation myths, which some scholars believe have different origins and which certainly have different emphases. These creation myths not only tell slightly different stories, but in places also contradict each other.

The first account - Genesis 1

1 In the beginning God created the heavens and the earth. 2 Now the earth was formless and empty, darkness was over the surface of the deep, and the Spirit of God was hovering over the waters.

3 And God said, "Let there be light", and there was light. 4 God saw that the light was good, and he separated the light from the darkness. 5 God called the light "day", and the darkness he called "night". And there was evening, and there was morning - the first day.

6 And God said, "Let there be a vault between the waters to separate water from water." 7 So God made the vault and separated the water under the vault from the water above it. And it was so. 8 God called the vault "sky". And there was evening, and there was morning - the second day.

9 And God said, "Let the water under the sky be gathered to one place, and let dry ground appear." And it was so. 10 God called the dry ground "land", and the gathered waters he called "seas". And God saw that it was good.

11 Then God said, "Let the land produce vegetation: seed-bearing plants and trees on the land that bear fruit with seed in it, according to their various kinds." And it was so. 12 The land produced vegetation: plants bearing seed according to their kinds and trees bearing fruit with seed in it according to their kinds. And God saw that it was good. 13 And there was evening, and there was morning - the third day.

14 And God said, "Let there be lights in the vault of the sky to separate the day from the night, and let them serve as signs to mark sacred times, and days and years, 15 and let them be lights in the vault of the sky to give light on the earth." And it was so. 16 God made two great lights - the greater light to govern the day and the lesser light to govern the night. He also made the stars. 17 God set them in the vault of the sky to give light on the earth, 18 to govern the day and the night, and to separate light from darkness. And God saw

that it was good. 19 And there was evening, and there was morning - the fourth day.

20 And God said, "Let the water teem with living creatures, and let birds fly above the earth across the vault of the sky." 21 So God created the great creatures of the sea and every living thing with which the water teems and that moves about in it, according to their kinds, and every winged bird according to its kind. And God saw that it was good. 22 God blessed them and said, "Be fruitful and increase in number and fill the water in the seas, and let the birds increase on the earth." 23 And there was evening, and there was morning - the fifth day.

24 And God said, "Let the land produce living creatures according to their kinds: the livestock, the creatures that move along the ground, and the wild animals, each according to its kind." And it was so. 25 God made the wild animals according to their kinds, the livestock according to their kinds, and all the creatures that move along the ground according to their kinds. And God saw that it was good.

26 Then God said, "Let us make mankind in our image, in our likeness, so that they may rule over the fish in the sea and the birds in the sky, over the livestock and all the wild animals, and over all the creatures that move along the ground."

27 So God created mankind in his own image, in the image of God he created them; male and female he created them.

28 God blessed them and said to them, "Be fruitful and increase in number; fill the earth and subdue it. Rule over the fish in the sea and the birds in the sky and over every living creature that moves on the ground."

29 Then God said, "I give you every seed-bearing plant on the face of the whole earth and every tree that has fruit with seed in it. They will be yours for food. 30 And to all the beasts of the earth and all the birds in the sky and all the creatures that move along the ground - everything that has the breath of life in it - I give every green plant for food." And it was so.

31 God saw all that he had made, and it was very good. And there was evening, and there was morning - the sixth day.

32 Thus the heavens and the earth were completed in all their vast array.

33 By the seventh day God had finished the work he had been doing; so on the seventh day he rested from all his work. 34 Then God blessed the seventh day and made it holy, because on it he rested from all the work of creating that he had done.

The purpose of this account is usually taken to be that it maps out creation; it gives a scheme for how the universe was made. God does not craft the universe in this account like a sculptor; He seemingly speaks the universe into existence. He says "Let there be light" and, as we hear, "there was light" (Gen 1:3). As we hear in the words of hymn-writer John Mason:

Thou spak'st, and Heav'n and Earth appear'd,
And answer'd to thy Call;
As if their Maker's Voice they heard,
Which is the Creatures' all.

The world begins to exist not at God's action, but at His word. Perhaps this emphasises God's power, that matter itself could be formed through speech; perhaps it shows how His creation is incomparable to things that humans craft or create.

The creation of the world, according to Genesis 1, happens over six days. On each day, a different stage of creation is completed. When each thing is complete, it is said that "God saw that it was good" (Genesis 1:3, 10, 12, 18, 21, 25 and finally 31). God is therefore a being that creates in order to achieve goodness; He wills a good world into existence. This tells us not only of His goodness but also His power, as He is both willing and able to create a good world.

The order of creation in Genesis 1 is important. He creates things on the grand scale first, creating light, the sky and the sea. He creates dry ground, and then plants, birds and fish, land animals and finally humankind. When His creation is complete, it says that "on the seventh day he rested". In Judaism seven is symbolic of perfection and completeness. Perhaps this symbolism comes from this story, or perhaps the story is written in this way to emphasise this symbolism; we cannot know for sure. Still, on the seventh day of creation, we are presented with God's creation, which He speaks into existence, and which He sees as good; complete.

The second narrative - Genesis 2-3

The account of creation that takes place in the second and third chapters of Genesis is somewhat different in its emphasis:

4 This is the account of the heavens and the earth when they were created, when the Lord God made the earth and the heavens.

5 Now no shrub had yet appeared on the earth and no plant had yet sprung up, for the Lord God had not sent rain on the earth and there was no one to work the ground, 6 but streams came up from the earth and watered the whole surface of the ground. 7 Then the Lord God formed a man from the dust of the ground and breathed into his nostrils the breath of life, and the man became a living being.

8 Now the Lord God had planted a garden in the east, in Eden; and there he put the man he had formed. 9 The Lord God made all kinds of trees grow out of the ground - trees that were pleasing to the eye and good for food. In the middle of the garden were the tree of life and the tree of the knowledge of good and evil.

10 A river watering the garden flowed from Eden; from there it was separated into four headwaters. 11 The name of the first is the Pishon; it winds through the entire land of Havilah, where there is gold. 12 (The gold of that land is good; aromatic resin and onyx are also there.) 13 The name of the second river is the Gihon; it winds through the entire land of Cush. 14 The name of the third river is the Tigris; it runs along the east side of Ashur. And the fourth river is the Euphrates.

15 The Lord God took the man and put him in the Garden of Eden to work it and take care of it. 16 And the Lord God commanded the man, "You are free to eat from any tree in the garden; 17 but you must not eat from the tree of the knowledge of good and evil, for when you eat from it you will certainly die."

18 The Lord God said, "It is not good for the man to be alone. I will make a helper suitable for him."

19 Now the Lord God had formed out of the ground all the wild animals and all the birds in the sky. He brought them to the man to see what he would name them; and whatever the man called each living creature, that was its name. 20 So the man gave names to all the livestock, the birds in the sky and all the wild animals.

But for Adam no suitable helper was found. 21 So the Lord God caused the man to fall into a deep sleep; and while he was sleeping, he took one of the man's ribs and then closed up the place with flesh. 22 Then the Lord God made a woman from the rib he had taken out of the man, and he brought her to the man.

23 The man said,

"This is now bone of my bones
*   and flesh of my flesh;*
she shall be called 'woman,'
*   for she was taken out of man."*

24 That is why a man leaves his father and mother and is united to his wife, and they become one flesh.

25 Adam and his wife were both naked, and they felt no shame.

3 Now the serpent was more crafty than any of the wild animals the Lord God had made. He said to the woman, "Did God really say, 'You must not eat from any tree in the garden'?"

2 The woman said to the serpent, "We may eat fruit from the trees in the garden", 3 but God did say, "You must not eat fruit from the tree that is in the middle of the garden, and you must not touch it, or you will die."

4 "You will not certainly die," the serpent said to the woman. 5 "For God knows that when you eat from it your eyes will be opened, and you will be like God, knowing good and evil."

6 When the woman saw that the fruit of the tree was good for food and pleasing to the eye, and also desirable for gaining wisdom, she took some and ate it. She also gave some to her husband, who was with her, and he ate it. 7 Then the eyes of both of them were opened, and they realised they were naked; so they sewed fig leaves together and made coverings for themselves.

8 Then the man and his wife heard the sound of the Lord God as he was walking in the garden in the cool of the day, and they hid from the Lord God among the trees of the garden. 9 But the Lord God called to the man, "Where are you?"

10 He answered, "I heard you in the garden, and I was afraid because I was naked; so I hid."

11 And he said, "Who told you that you were naked? Have you eaten from the tree that I commanded you not to eat from?"

12 The man said, "The woman you put here with me - she gave me some fruit from the tree, and I ate it."

13 Then the Lord God said to the woman, "What is this you have done?"

The woman said, "The serpent deceived me, and I ate."

14 So the Lord God said to the serpent, "Because you have done this,

Cursed are you above all livestock
  and all wild animals!
You will crawl on your belly
  and you will eat dust
  all the days of your life.
15 And I will put enmity
  between you and the woman,
  and between your offspring and hers;
he will crush your head,
  and you will strike his heel."

16 To the woman he said,

"I will make your pains in childbearing very severe;
  with painful labour you will give birth to children.
Your desire will be for your husband,
  and he will rule over you."

17 To Adam he said, "Because you listened to your wife and ate fruit from the tree about which I commanded you, 'You must not eat from it,'

"Cursed is the ground because of you;
  through painful toil you will eat food from it
  all the days of your life.
18 It will produce thorns and thistles for you
  and you will eat the plants of the field.
19 By the sweat of your brow
  you will eat your food
until you return to the ground,
  since from it you were taken;
for dust you are
  and to dust you will return."

20 Adam named his wife Eve, because she would become the mother of all the living.

21 The Lord God made garments of skin for Adam and his wife and clothed them. 22 And the Lord God said, "The man has now become like one of us, knowing good and evil. He must not be allowed to reach out his hand and take also from the tree of life and eat, and live

forever." 23 So the Lord God banished him from the Garden of Eden to work the ground from which he had been taken. 24 After he drove the man out, he placed on the east side of the Garden of Eden cherubim and a flaming sword flashing back and forth to guard the way to the tree of life.

Rather than depicting creation on the cosmic scale, this story emphasises humanity's place in creation, and the relationship between God and humankind. This is the familiar tale of Adam and Eve in the Garden of Eden, and their disobedience of God's only command, not to eat the fruit from the Tree of the Knowledge of Good and Evil. In this account, we see, perhaps, a more noticeably **ANTHROPOMORPHIC** God: one that walks; one that enters into conversation with people; one that physically sculpts aspects of creation. The Genesis 2-3 account is not interested in how the universe comes about; it starts with a world devoid of animals or plants, but does not explain how the world got there.

This story is more about humanity's role within the created world. Adam is put in charge of the other creatures and each animal is brought to him to be named. Unlike Genesis 1, in which God makes "male and female" humans at the same time, in Genesis 2, Eve is created to be a "helper" for Adam, and is made from one of Adam's ribs. Many have commented that this suggests that women are seen in this story to be subordinate to men, but one possible interpretation of "helper" is that it is more like a person without whom it is impossible to function, rather than a glorified personal assistant!

There are two trees in the centre of the Garden of Eden: one is the Tree of Life, and one is the Tree of the Knowledge of Good and Evil. God commands that Adam and Eve should not eat from the Tree of the Knowledge of Good and Evil. In fact, God commands this before the creation of Eve, but when Eve talks to the serpent, it is clear that she is aware that this is something she is not allowed to do.

The Tree of the Knowledge of Good and Evil might be named such because it symbolises the limits that humanity should have to their knowledge. As the serpent says to Eve, their ignorance is what separates mankind from God "for God knows that when you eat from it your eyes will be opened, and you will be like God, knowing good and evil". (Genesis 2:5) To be in Eden then, is a state of literally blissful ignorance; the boundaries of which humans, with their curious ways were, perhaps, bound to push.

The serpent persuades Eve to eat the fruit, and she in turn gives the fruit to Adam. Suddenly, their eyes are indeed opened, and they realise that they are naked. They hear God walking in the Garden, and hide from Him in shame. The fact that they know that they are naked means that God knows His commandment has been broken; Adam and Eve are no longer innocent. He curses them and banishes them from paradise.

Unlike Genesis 1, which aims to explain the origin of the universe, Genesis 2-3 has a clear moral. The Adam and Eve narrative tells us of humanity's relationship with God, and the difference between God and humankind. It tells us the origins of evil, both immorality and suffering.

So, we have here two quite different accounts of creation. Let us summarise the main differences.

Creation of the universe

GENESIS 1 - THE SIX-DAY CREATION MYTH

God is a creator on a cosmic scale. God brings light out of darkness and sets up sky and land.

GENESIS 2-3 - ADAM AND EVE AND THE FALL OF MAN

The first stage we hear about is that no plant has sprouted from the earth; the creation of the world itself is not explained here.

The method of creation

GENESIS 1 - THE SIX-DAY CREATION MYTH

God speaks, and the world appears. He is not spoken of crafting or sculpting, but seems to be a different kind of creator.

GENESIS 2-3 - ADAM AND EVE AND THE FALL OF MAN

God is more of an anthropomorphic deity, who forms Adam from the dust of the ground and creates Eve out of one of Adam's ribs.

The order of creation

GENESIS 1 - THE SIX-DAY CREATION MYTH

Creation begins on the cosmic scale, then life is created from the least complex to the most complex.

God creates:

- *Light*

- *Day and night*

- *Sky*

- *Water*

- *Dry ground separate from seas*

- *Plants*

- *Sun and Moon*

- *Birds and fish*

- *Land-dwelling creatures*

- *Humans (in His own image), male and female at the same time*

GENESIS 2-3 - ADAM AND EVE AND THE FALL OF MAN

The earth is dusty and empty because God had not yet caused the rains to come upon the land. God forms Adam out of the dust of the ground, and breathes life into him. God creates a garden, in the east, with all kinds of vegetation. He puts Adam there, and gives Adam the command that he can eat everything apart from the fruit from the Tree of the Knowledge of Good and Evil. God recognises that Adam needs not to be alone. He creates animals and brings them to Adam to name, but none of them is a suitable companion. He causes Adam to fall into a deep sleep, and forms Eve out of one of Adam's ribs. Adam calls her "bone of my bones and flesh of my flesh", and names her "'woman' because she was taken out of man". (Gen 2:23)

The role of humanity

GENESIS 1 - THE SIX-DAY CREATION MYTH

Humanity is created "in God's image". This shows that humans are in some way God-like, and that they are the pinnacle of creation. It is after the creation of humans that God's creation is complete. Humans are put in charge of creation (some translations suggest that humanity is in control of it, like a king; some suggest that it is more like a shepherd or custodian, taking care of creation).

GENESIS 2-3 - ADAM AND EVE AND THE FALL OF MAN

This is a story with a moral that is all about the role of humanity within creation. Humanity seems to be central. In this story, Adam is the first thing to be created, and then the Garden of Eden is created as a paradise for him to live in. Animals are created to be company for him, and he gets to name them. Eve is made for the benefit of Adam. Everything centres around Adam. But the moral is that given the creation of a perfect world, humanity always strives for more, and breaks the only commandment given to them. Ignorance was blissful, but humanity chose painful awareness instead.

The emphasis of the narrative

GENESIS 1 - THE SIX-DAY CREATION MYTH

The emphasis seems to be on God's great creative power, that He speaks a universe into existence. Although humanity is the culmination of creation and hence clearly of great importance in the story, this is not really a narrative with a moral as such.

GENESIS 2-3 - ADAM AND EVE AND THE FALL OF MAN

This story has at its centre a moral. Unlike Genesis 1, which is an explanatory narrative, Genesis 2 seems to be less concerned with describing the whole process of creation; it does not even mention how the earth got there. The point of this story is the relationship between Man and God, and the origin of evil.

God's role as a creator is not reflected only in Genesis, where the accounts of creation are given, but it is a theme that emerges again and again in scripture.

God as a craftsman

In Psalm 119:73, it is said of God that "Thy hands have made me and fashioned me: give me understanding, that I may learn thy commandments." Here we see an image that appears again and again in the Old Testament; the idea of God as a craftsman. This is perhaps more in line with the imagery used in Genesis 2, rather than Genesis 1, as Genesis 1 concerns itself with creation on a grand scale. Often, God is depicted as a potter, and humanity, by extension, is the clay. Let us look at some examples of this image of God as a craftsman.

BIBLE REFERENCE	WHAT IS SAID
Genesis 2:7	*Then the LORD God formed a man from the dust of the ground and breathed into his nostrils the breath of life, and the man became a living being.*
Psalm 8:3-4	*When I consider your heavens,* 　*the work of your fingers,* *the moon and the stars,* 　*which you have set in place,* *what is mankind that you are mindful of them,* 　*human beings that you care for them?*
Psalm 104:5-6	*You set the earth on its foundations, so that it shall never be shaken. You cover it with the deep as with a garment; the waters stood above the mountains.*
Psalm 119:73	*Thy hands have made me and fashioned me: give me understanding, that I may learn thy commandments.*

BIBLE REFERENCE	WHAT IS SAID

Job 38:4-7	Where were you when I laid the earth's foundation?
	    Tell me, if you understand.
	Who marked off its dimensions?
	    Surely you know!
	Who stretched a measuring line across it?
	    On what were its footings set, or who laid its cornerstone -
	    while the morning stars sang together
	and all the angels shouted for joy?

Isaiah 29:16	You turn things upside down,
	    as if the potter were thought to be like the clay!
	Shall what is formed say to the one who formed it,
	    "You did not make me"?
	Can the pot say to the potter,
	    "You know nothing"?

Isaiah 40:28	"The Lord is the everlasting God, the Creator of the ends of the earth. He does not faint or grow weary; his understanding is unsearchable."

Isaiah 64:8	Yet you, Lord, are our Father.
	    We are the clay, you are the potter;
	    we are all the work of your hand.

The image of God as a craftsman has implications beyond the idea of creative power. Of course, God's skills of craftsmanship show great intelligence, as well as care about His creation, but there is more to it than that. Often, the image of God as a craftsman is used specifically of humanity; He crafted us. In some passages, such as Psalm 8, this is used to emphasise how extraordinary it is that humanity should matter to God; the Psalmist was clearly struck by awe at his insignificance in the grand scheme of things.

In other passages, it seems as though humanity's status as created beings is being emphasised in order to make a point about God's power, and more specifically His status over us. In Isaiah 29, we see the image of humans as being like the clay, and the memorable image of the clay questioning the potter. The message is clear: as created beings, we cannot question our creator. This is made even more explicit in the story of Job, where Job is finding it impossible to understand why he is suffering. Job has always obeyed the law, and been very careful not to do anything wrong; he cannot think of a sin that deserves the suffering he has endured. God speaks to Job "in a storm" (you can tell He is angry) and asks Job if he was there when God beat out the vault of the heavens. In other words, an understanding of the workings of the universe can only come when you are its creator.

GOD AND CREATION IN THE NEW TESTAMENT

You might think that the theme of God as a creator would not appear in the New Testament. After all, the Torah begins with two creation stories, and Christianity adopted the Torah into what they called The Old Testament.

But it is not the initial creation of the world that is being talked about in the New Testament, but a "new creation" that comes because of Jesus' death and resurrection. This new creation is prophesied in the Old Testament in Isaiah 65:17, where God says "I will create new heavens and a new earth. The former things will not be remembered, nor will they come to mind." The message of Christianity is one of renewal and new hope for the future. As it says in 2 Peter 3:13 "we are looking forward to a new heaven and a new earth, where righteousness dwells". This new heaven and new earth is usually associated with the coming of the Kingdom of Heaven at the end of time. As it says in the last book of the Bible, Revelation 21:1-3, which foresees the end of the world,

> Then I saw a new heaven and a new earth, for the first heaven and the first earth had passed away, and there was no longer any sea. 2 I saw the Holy City, the new Jerusalem, coming down out of heaven from God, prepared as a bride beautifully dressed for her husband. 3 And I heard a loud voice from the throne saying, "Look! God's dwelling place is now among the people, and he will dwell with them. They will be his people, and God himself will be with them and be their God."

God's creative power is not, therefore, a one-time event. In the Old Testament, God creates the world. In the New Testament, God makes the world anew. The depiction of God in the Bible is unlike Aristotle's Prime Mover, who is uninvolved and unaware of his creation. This is a God that creates, sustains and recreates, and renews the world.

A TRUE ACCOUNT OF CREATION?

Creationism is a view of the Bible that holds Genesis to be a literally true account of creation. Many wrongly assume that literal belief in the Bible is very old, but actually, it is a relatively new worldview.

In the 17th C, Archbishop James Ussher compiled his so-called "chronology" of the Bible. From working through each character in the Bible, and when they were reported to have died, Ussher attempted to calculate the precise time and date of creation. Ussher traced creation back to a Sunday in October in 4004 BC. In other words, he would think that the world today is around 6,000 years old.

This was not however incorporated as a mainstream view in Christianity. Ussher's understanding of creation did not in fact receive popularity until a trend for literalism grew in the 19th C, especially in America after the Civil War. Particularly in the southern states, creationism became a dominant view and remains so to this day.

In the early part of the 20th C, creationism went from strength to strength, especially as a response to fears about the implications of evolution. Many people felt that evolution was a harsh cruel process, and that had certain sociological implications. If evolution, rather than God, was the creative and guiding principle in nature, what value would those with physical learning disabilities or mental health problems have? Evolution favours those well suited to their environments, and there is no place for anyone else.

One of the areas where evolution has frequently caused controversy in the southern states is its place in education. Social Darwinism was feared, and some were very fearful of this harmful worldview being fed to their children. This reached a peak in the 1920s in the **SCOPES TRIAL**, where a young teacher called John Scopes was prosecuted for teaching evolution in class. The trial became a foil for a more general discussion of evolution and creationism. Scopes was found guilty and fined.

This fear of so-called **SOCIAL DARWINISM** seems to have been borne out with some of the atrocities committed during the Second World War in Nazi concentration camps, where those with learning disabilities and mental health problems were often sterilised or euthanised. Creationism gave a pleasanter view; a God that set up a world that He saw to be "good"; one where everything is part of a loved creation.

Creationism is still a dominant view in the southern states to this day. In Gallup polls from between 1982 and 2012, the number of Americans polled who believe that God created mankind as we are now, rather than believing in evolution, has remained fairly constant at 40-47%. In 2012, it was 46%. Nearly half of Americans, then, believe the Genesis accounts of creation to be true.

REASONS TO DISMISS CREATIONISM

Creationism is, however, extremely controversial, amongst Christians as well as non-believers. There are four main reasons for this.

1. Creationism is not a mainstream Christian view, and never has been

Many Christians dismiss creationism as a misunderstanding of the role of the Bible within their faith. The Bible is important, but is not important because it is a book of answers. Traditionally, the Roman Catholic Church and more Catholic elements in the Anglican tradition have understood the Bible as being part of the picture, but that human reason and the authority of the Church also has a part to play. Many Christians would say that the Bible conveys spiritual truth, not literal truth. To mistake Genesis for an account of the creation of the world is to miss the point.

2. The stories make no sense if they are taken literally

It can also be argued that the Genesis creation accounts cannot support a literal interpretation. For a start, as we said earlier, there are not one but two accounts, which contradict each other. If we were to believe in the literal truth of these stories, should we believe that man was created first (as in Genesis 2) or last (as in Genesis 1)? Were humans created, male and female, at the same time, or was Eve taken from Adam's side? It is impossible to believe that both accounts are literally true, because it would mean believing things that are inconsistent; that contradict each other.

Moreover, the Genesis 1 account is not even consistent within itself: there was light before there was a sun and moon; there were days before the sun and moon were in the sky. A literal reading of Genesis 1 simply does not add up. A better understanding might be that it is intended as a poetic explanation for the origins of the world; one that expresses God's power and goodness. The style of writing would support this hypothesis, as Hebrew poetry uses a lot of repetition. This would explain the fact that we see the phrases "and there was evening, and there was morning" and "He saw that it was good" appearing throughout the chapter.

3. There is a huge weight of evidence in favour of evolution

Evolutionary biologists would also suggest that the evidence for the world being 6,000 years old is pretty thin. There are fossils of dinosaurs that contemporary dating methods have shown to be millions of years old. Creationists might deny the validity of the methods of dating these fossils; indeed, in the Creation Museum in Kansas, it is possible to see displays of dinosaurs playing with children; they believe that dinosaurs were created along with the other land creatures that God made just before humans on day six. Hence, they would say that the fossils are 6,000 years old, not millions of years old. This is, however, little more than an assertion based on their prior assumption that the world is only 6,000 years old; dating methods used by scientists to establish the age of fossils are well established. There is no reason to think that dinosaurs lived 6,000 years ago unless you already believe that the world did not exist before then.

4. A richer religious significance comes from reading the narratives metaphorically

If the Genesis creation accounts are both taken as literal, we are faced with two stories that contradict each other, and in places seem confused in themselves. They would also require for us to reject well-established scientific hypotheses with very little evidence. On the other hand, if we read them for their religious meaning, and not a literal one, we might find that we get more from them.

Genesis 1 tells us about the nature of God. The fact that He can speak a world into existence shows His great power. The fact that He "saw that it was good" shows that He set the world up to be perfect; He is a good God, and concerned to create a good world. This is a God that does not simply make the world, but is involved with it and cares about it.

Genesis 2 tells us about God as a source of morality and a law giver. It tells us that creation from God was perfect, but it was humanity's curiosity that destroyed it. It tells us about humanity's arrogance; wanting to know and understand everything. It tells us of humanity's presumption to ignore their maker in disobeying His only command.

DID THE GOD OF THE BIBLE CREATE EX NIHILO?

As we said before, the God of classical theism is held to have created ex nihilo, but it is not clear whether this is how things are depicted in the Bible. There is some evidence to suggest that God created out of something pre-existing, but there is also good reason to think God created out of nothing. We are going to examine the evidence on both sides of the argument.

If God did not create ex nihilo (out of nothing), He created ex materia (out of matter). Clearly, to create a world from nothing is a greater act of power than to sculpt it from what was already in existence.

The case against creation ex nihilo

Let us go back to the beginning of Genesis. It says "In the beginning God created the heavens and the earth." So far, it seems that the account is compatible with believing God created ex nihilo, but look what happens in verse two: "Now the earth was formless and empty, darkness was over the surface of the deep, and the Spirit of God was hovering over the waters." This begs a number of questions:

- What is this formlessness, described in verse two?

- What is "the deep"? Where did it come from?

- How did the waters get there? There is no explanation of their creation, and seas are not created until later on.

WENHAM GORDON translates verse two as "Now the earth was total chaos ..."; **MARTIN KESSLER** translates it as "jumble and disorder". Perhaps the formless empty world indicates that there was a pre-existing chaos that God made into an ordered universe? In other words, perhaps this suggests that God created ex materia, making His creation one of bringing order rather than of originating.

Gordon suggests that the "darkness" is meant to contrast with God; after all, the first thing God says is "let there be light". God was often associated with light, and darkness, on the contrary, was everything that was ungodly. Perhaps we are being presented with a world that is unstructured, unlit, disordered and ungodly.

A lot hinges on how we read verse one of Genesis. Consider these options:

a) In the beginning, God made the heavens and the earth.

Now, the earth was formless and empty, darkness was over the surface of the deep, and the Spirit of God was hovering over the waters.

b) In the beginning, God made the heavens and the earth. Now, the earth was formless and empty, darkness was over the surface of the deep, and the Spirit of God was hovering over the waters.

If we take verse one to be a title, as in option a), it seems we have to conclude that God did not create ex nihilo. If, on the other hand, verse one is not a title, then it could be saying that He made the heavens and the earth out of nothing, but that initially that creation was formless, and dark, and God had to bring order and light into the world. This could be seen as problematic, however, as "the deep" and "the waters" are never specifically mentioned as having been created.

No evidence so far has categorically shown that God did not create ex nihilo, but the unexplained existence of this chaotic world with "waters" and "the deep" might prove problematic for someone who holds that the God of the Bible creates ex nihilo.

The case for creation ex nihilo

We have examined the evidence that might suggest that God creates ex materia. Now let us look at reasons to argue the other point of view. We will largely do this by looking at what words are being used in the original Hebrew.

There are different words that can be used to mean "create" in Hebrew: The word asah can be translated as "make", whereas bara is often translated "create" and yasar is often translated as "form". So, to put it simply, you would asah a cake; bringing lots of things together to make something else. You would yasar a sculpture, or a piece of pottery; it is a process of formation.

The word bara appears again and again in Genesis 1. Interestingly, though, you could not bara anything, because bara is a term used, as **YATES** and **WALTKE** point out, only of God. You and I can make and form, but it seems only God can create. There is, therefore something very special about what God does when He creates.

Many scholars, including **VINE** and **HENRY**, have taken this linguistic phenomenon, this word that only applies to God, as evidence that God created ex nihilo. It is certain that bara implies creation, as Vine notes, "on a cosmic scale".

Others are more reticent to claim that the word bara implies creation ex nihilo. **ALLEN P ROSS** argues that bara emphasises that the creation is new and perfect, but does not necessarily have to come from nothing. **WENHAM GORDON** goes as far as to say that bara does not imply creation from nothing, because the verb can be applied to, for example the creation of Israel, which did not come from nothing.

CONCLUSION

In the debate about whether the God of the Bible creates from nothing, there is good evidence on either side. If God did create ex nihilo, where did "the waters" come from? But at the same time, why use a special verb for God's creative actions if they are not different from other acts of creation? The cases made by both sides are plausible, but neither is conclusive, and so it is difficult to know for certain whether the God of the Bible is depicted as creating ex nihilo or ex materia.

God's goodness

KEY TERMS

COVENANT - A promise made by God to his people, in exchange for their obedience.

DIVINE COMMAND THEORY - The view supported by Søren Kirkegaard, amongst others, that God's command is what makes something good.

EUTHYPHRO DILEMMA - Raised in Plato's Euthyphro, it is a dilemma surrounding the origin of goodness; whether God prescribes something because it is good, or whether something is good by virtue of the fact that God prescribes it.

FORM OF THE GOOD - Plato's idea of the highest summit of reality; the Form of the Good is the highest good; all other good derives from it.

NEO-PLATONISTS - Thinkers coming after Plato, who are heavily influenced by him and adopt many of his ideas.

NEW COVENANT - A new promise made by God through Jesus of redemption to all people through belief in Christ.

The goodness of God is core to the Christian view of God. So much so, in fact that many encapsulate His nature by saying "God is love". Yet God's goodness is also one of the most emotive and controversial issues in the Philosophy of Religion.

In this chapter:

- What do we mean by "good"? (AS + A2)

- God's goodness (AS + A2)

- God's goodness in the Bible (AS)

- Problems with God's goodness? (AS)

- Is something good because God commands it, or does God command it because it is good? (AS)

- Can a good God reward and punish? (A2)

WHAT DO WE MEAN BY "GOOD"?

One reason that there is so much difficulty with God's goodness is because "good" is an extremely broad term, used in many different ways. When we say God is "good", what precisely do we mean? Take the following uses of the word "good".

- A good person

- A good book

- A good policeman

- A good fight

- A good telling off

- A good judge

All of these are natural uses of the word "good" in English, and when we use them in speech, we are not particularly worried that they might have different senses; we navigate the subtleties of our language with relative ease most of the time. Yet, as **AQUINAS** points out in his discussion of religious language, when words have more than one meaning (when they equivocate), the sense of what it meant might be lost. So we need to be very clear what sense of "good" we are referring to when we analyse the concept of God's goodness.

What senses of good are there? Let's look through the list.

A GOOD PERSON - Someone moral; ethically good; someone with good character traits.

A GOOD BOOK - A book that is excellent amongst books - one that is entertaining, perhaps, or has high literary and aesthetic merit.

A GOOD POLICEMAN - Someone who upholds the law and acts against crime.

A GOOD FIGHT - A fight that perhaps is worth seeing, so one that is entertaining, or a fight where opponents are evenly matched, so the fight requires skill, not only force.

A GOOD TELLING OFF - A reproach that is effective; perhaps because it stops someone continuing down a bad route.

A GOOD JUDGE - Someone who makes wise and just decisions and punishes people for misdeeds.

We can immediately see that the word "good" is being used in such different ways that it might lead to contradiction. The most obvious example of this is the example of the good fight. The fight might be good in the sense of being really evenly matched and nail-biting to watch. However, it could also be conducted illegally and involve a lot of violence. The fight would good in one sense, and bad in other senses.

Given that "good" is used in such contrasting contexts and for such different things, we should ask what, if anything, these things have in common. One response that we could give is that all of the things we have described are excellent instances of a particular thing: a good fight might not be morally good, but it is an excellent instance of a fight; a good book might have characters we disapprove of, but it is excellent as a piece of literature; a good telling off might be unpleasant, but it is an effective reproach and deterrent.

GOD'S GOODNESS

To talk of God as good might be to talk of His excellence; His perfection. This would certainly coincide with how many philosophers describe God. **DESCARTES** conceives of God as a perfect being; something superior to anything else. **AQUINAS** argues in the fourth of his "five ways" that a supremely excellent being must exist in order to explain lesser goods we observe in the world. **ANSELM**, in Chapter 5 of the Proslogion, writes"

> ... what are you, except that which, as the highest of all beings, alone exists through itself, and creates all other things from nothing? ... What good, therefore, does the supreme Good lack, through which every good is? Therefore, you are just, truthful, blessed, and whatever it is better to be than not to be. For it is better to be just than not just; better to be blessed than not blessed. - Anselm, Proslogion, Ch. 5

Just as all our other examples of "good" describe an instance of excellence, so we can talk of God's goodness as "excellence". But goodness is not just a quality God is said to have. As **ANSELM** says, He is "the highest of all beings". God is perfectly good; He is omnibenevolent. God's goodness is "supreme" and every other good comes from His goodness, so perhaps God's goodness is not an excellence, but excellence itself. On this view, God is not perfect; He is perfection.

NEO-PLATONISTS (philosophers after Plato who were influenced by his views) often equated the **FORM OF THE GOOD** with God. Plato's idea of the Form of the Good was the ultimate reality; the pinnacle of existence at which all philosophers should aim. The idea of goodness being God's very nature chimes very much, therefore with a view influenced by platonic thought, and platonic influences in Christian thinking.

GOD'S GOODNESS IN THE BIBLE

We have said that the term "good" is used in many different ways, and there are different facets to the presentation of God's goodness in the Bible.

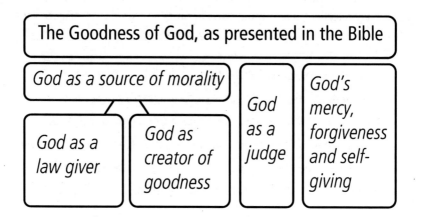

These dimensions of God's goodness are quite different from each other, and potentially in conflict. In the Old Testament, God is spoken of as, on the one hand, "righteous" (tzedek), mishpat and din (which both mean "just"), and, on the other hand, as good (tov), gracious (channun), showing loving kindness (chesed) and compassion (rachamin). **GOLDBERG AND RAYNER** suggest that God is shown as much to be a righteous God as a gracious one; as just as He is compassionate. These are two very different aspects of divine goodness.

God as a source of morality - the creator of goodness

In the Bible, God is presented as the source of goodness. The first evidence of this comes in the first chapter of Genesis when God creates the world. After creating each thing, "God saw that it was good". This is a God who is creating not just any world, but a good world. Furthermore, if we think Genesis depicts creation ex nihilo, (see the chapter on God as creator) God would not simply be forming a good world from pre-existent matter, but would be creating goodness from nothing; he would be constructing the goodness of the world just as He constructs everything else in it. As it says in one of the prayers in the Book of Common Prayer, it is "God, from whom all holy desires, all good counsels, and all just works do proceed"; goodness comes from Him.

God as a source of morality - a law giver

The idea that God is a source of morality is made more concrete by the fact that he is a **LAW GIVER**. God is not simply the creator of goodness, but He prescribes certain actions and sets standards of human behaviour. One of the main themes that characterises the Jewish tradition is the idea of God's law; it being mankind's responsibility to live up to the values He sets. One could say that the core question in the Old Testament is that posed in Deuteronomy:

> And now Israel, what does the Lord your God require of you? (Deut. 10:12)

The first place we see God giving commandments is in the story of the Fall of Man, where God sets but one command (that Adam and Eve must not eat the fruit from the Tree of the Knowledge of Good and Evil), which is soon broken, and leads to the expulsion of Adam and Eve from the Garden of Eden. The story of Adam and Eve is primarily about God's relationship with humanity, and its focus is really a moral one. God puts Adam and Eve into a paradise and issues one command, but yet they cannot keep it.

Later on in Genesis (Genesis 22), we find a command that is hard to understand. God commands Abraham to sacrifice his son, Isaac. Abraham responds with faith to God's command, and goes to perform the sacrifice unquestioningly, despite the unthinkable demand God has placed on him. When Isaac asks where the animal for the sacrifice is, Abraham responds that God will provide it. Before Abraham goes to kill his son, God halts the sacrifice. Abraham sees a ram caught by its horns in a thicket, which he uses instead. God did, indeed provide the sacrifice. Many see this as an exemplar of how people should respond to God's commands; with faith and without questioning.

In Exodus, Moses has leads the Israelites away from slavery in Egypt and is taking them to freedom in the Promised Land. God speaks to Moses on Mount Sinai; His voice is accompanied by cloud, smoke and lightning. In Chapter 20, God gives to Moses (and through him the rest of the Israelites) the Ten Commandments, which are sometimes known in the Christian tradition as the Decalogue (from the Greek words for "ten statements").

ORIGEN (living in the 2nd and 3rd centuries CE) notes that in Egypt, God sent down Ten Plagues on the Israelites' captors; now God sends down Ten Commandments to His chosen people:

> *2 I am the Lord thy God, which have brought thee out of the land of Egypt, out of the house of bondage.*

> *3 Thou shalt have no other gods before me.*

> *4 Thou shalt not make unto thee any graven image, or any likeness of any thing that is in heaven above, or that is in the earth beneath, or that is in the water under the earth: 5 thou shalt not bow down thyself*

to them, nor serve them: for I the Lord thy God am a jealous God,
visiting the iniquity of the fathers upon the children unto the third and
fourth generation of them that hate me; 6 and showing mercy unto
thousands of them that love me, and keep my commandments.

7 Thou shalt not take the name of the Lord thy God in vain; for
the Lord will not hold him guiltless that taketh his name in vain.

8 Remember the sabbath day, to keep it holy. 9 Six days shalt thou
labour, and do all thy work: 10 but the seventh day is the sabbath of
the Lord thy God: in it thou shalt not do any work, thou, nor thy son,
nor thy daughter, thy manservant, nor thy maidservant, nor thy cattle,
nor thy stranger that is within thy gates: 11 for in six days
the Lord made heaven and earth, the sea, and all that in them is, and
rested the seventh day: wherefore the Lord blessed the sabbath day,
and hallowed it.

12 Honour thy father and thy mother: that thy days may be long upon
the land which the Lord thy God giveth thee.

13 Thou shalt not kill.

14 Thou shalt not commit adultery.

15 Thou shalt not steal.

16 Thou shalt not bear false witness against thy neighbour.

17 Thou shalt not covet thy neighbour's house, thou shalt not covet

thy neighbour's wife, nor his manservant, nor his maidservant, nor his
ox, nor his ass, nor any thing that is thy neighbour's.

(Exodus 20:2-17, Authorised Version)

The numbering of the Ten Commandments has been controversial. In the Jewish tradition, they treat verse 2 as its own commandment; in the Roman Catholic tradition, they treat verses 2-6 as one commandment. I will be using the common numbering used in the Anglican tradition, largely because it seems the easiest reading of the text:

1. *I am the Lord thy God, which have brought thee out of the land*
    of Egypt, out of the house of bondage. Thou shalt have no other
    gods before me.

2. *Thou shalt not make unto thee any graven image, or any*
    likeness of any thing that is in heaven above, or that is in the
    earth beneath, or that is in the water under the earth

3. *Thou shalt not take the name of the Lord thy God in vain*

4. *Remember the sabbath day, to keep it holy*

5. *Honour thy father and thy mother*

6. *Thou shalt not kill*

7. *Thou shalt not commit adultery*

8. *Thou shalt not steal*

9. *Thou shalt not bear false witness against thy neighbour*

10. *Thou shalt not covet*

The commandments that perhaps stick best in our minds are the ones about not stealing, killing, not committing adultery and so on. Yet, the first four commandments are not about how the Israelites must behave towards each other, but how they must relate to God. The Ten Commandments form two sections: commandments about the treatment of God, and commandments about the treatment of others. The passage where we find these commandments is often taken in isolation, but it is part of a much longer declaration by God, where He talks precisely about what the implications of these commandments are. This longer tract is far longer and far more detailed than the passage containing the Ten Commandments, but like them contains not only moral imperatives but also religious ones.

God's commandments, both here and in the Old Testament in general, are often - wrongly - seen as a bit one-way. The common depiction of the event that has trickled down into popular consciousness is that God sits on high and tells the Israelites what to do. Of course, in a sense this is accurate, but it is missing an important dimension to understanding of God's law giving. God is not simply a distant deity that issues orders; He is said to have a **COVENANT** (a contract; a mutual promise) with the Israelites; His chosen people. As **GOLDBERG AND RAYNER** put it:

> ... the people ... are to be God's servants and witnesses, proclaiming
> His sovereignty, testifying to His unity, exemplifying His moral law, and
> so paving the way for the establishment of His kingdom, while He, on
> the condition of their continuing loyalty, will give them the instruction,
> the strength and the means ... to endure and carry out their
> assignment. - Goldberg and Rayner, The Jewish People, p274-275

In short, God's lawgiving is part of a relationship; He does not simply command, but supports and guides the Jewish people in keeping His commands. Here we see perhaps evidence of God's righteousness and mercy working alongside each other - this is not a God who is simply a judge and ruler but a support and strength to His people.

In the New Testament, a **NEW COVENANT** is established through Jesus, and a new law is given to mankind. When Jesus is asked what the greatest law is, He replies with what is known as the Shema Yisrael:

> *Hear, O Israel: The Lord our God, the Lord is one! You shall love the Lord your God with all your heart, with all your soul, and with all your strength. (Deuteronomy 6:4-5)*

Jesus also gives a new commandment; one that encapsulates the law. It has become known as "the Golden Rule" or "The Law of Love", and it commands

> *"Love your neighbour as yourself." There is no commandment greater than these. (Mark 12:31)*

Again, as in the Decalogue, Jesus maintains the sense that commandments are not just about how people relate to each other, but also how they relate to God. Jesus chooses two "great" commandments, to love God and to love your neighbour.

Again, as in the Old Testament, these commandments are not given in a context where God places Himself above humanity and issues demands. Emphasis is again placed on the relationship God has with humanity, and this is no more strongly felt than in God sending Jesus to walk and live amongst people. This is far from a law giver on high, because "God so loved the world that He gave His only begotten son that whosoever believes in Him will not perish but have everlasting life." (John 3:16) According to the message of Christianity, God is not just a law giver, but gives of Himself also for the benefit of humanity.

So, we see both in the Old Testament and the New Testament the role of God as a law giver, but it should not be understood simply that God is issuing commands, but that His laws demonstrate the relationship He has with His creation.

The role of God as judge

The corollary of God being the law giver is that He is also the judge; they go hand in hand. The teacher who sets homework is the one who marks it. They set the standard and so can measure homework against that standard. As it says in Psalm 75:

> It is God who judges:
> he brings one down, he exalts another. (Ps. 75:7)

In Genesis, when Adam and Eve eat the fruit from the Tree of the Knowledge of Good and Evil, God banishes them from paradise, and curses them. The man will now have to work the land in order to have food, and the woman will have pain in childhood and will be dominated by her husband. The serpent is to "crawl on its belly" (presumably it had legs when it tempted Eve?). Because of Adam and Eve, all of their descendants will now grow up outside the Garden of Eden.

Later in Genesis, we hear of Noah. Noah "found favour" with God, but the earth was so full of evil and wickedness (Genesis 6:5) that God was aggrieved and regretted having made humans. He decided to wipe them from the face of the earth. But God's judgement only applies to those who were wicked. Noah is commanded to build an ark that he, his wife, his sons and their wives, along with pairs of animals, will board before God sends the flood. In the flood, we see God's righteousness at work; He is blotting out all evil from His creation and saving only His faithful servants. At the end of the flood narrative, we see that God's righteousness is paired with mercy. He promises that He will never again destroy the whole earth.

The other key Old Testament story that tells of God's judgement is the destruction of Sodom and Gomorrah, where God rains down burning sulphur. We see here both God's justice and also His mercy in this dialogue between God and Abraham, when Abraham pleads with God to save the innocent.

Abraham remained standing before the Lord.

23 Then Abraham approached him and said: "Will you sweep away the righteous with the wicked?

24 What if there are fifty righteous people in the city? Will you really sweep it away and not spare the place for the sake of the fifty righteous people in it?

25 Far be it from you to do such a thing - to kill the righteous with the wicked, treating the righteous and the wicked alike. Far be it from you! Will not the Judge of all the earth do right?"

26 The Lord said, "If I find fifty righteous people in the city of Sodom, I will spare the whole place for their sake."

27 Then Abraham spoke up again: "Now that I have been so bold as to speak to the Lord, though I am nothing but dust and ashes,

28 what if the number of the righteous is five less than fifty? Will you destroy the whole city for lack of five people?"

"If I find forty-five there," he said, "I will not destroy it."

29 Once again he spoke to him, "What if only forty are found there?"

He said, "For the sake of forty, I will not do it."

30 Then he said, "May the Lord not be angry, but let me speak. What if only thirty can be found there?"

He answered, "I will not do it if I find thirty there."

31 Abraham said, "Now that I have been so bold as to speak to the Lord, what if only twenty can be found there?"

He said, "For the sake of twenty, I will not destroy it."

32 Then he said, "May the Lord not be angry, but let me speak just once more. What if only ten can be found there?"

He answered, "For the sake of ten, I will not destroy it."

33 When the Lord had finished speaking with Abraham, he left, and Abraham returned home.

We see that God would spare the whole city rather than punish those that don't deserve it. In fact, God saves four people from the destruction: Lot, his wife, and his two daughters.

Judgement in the New Testament

The stories we most associate with divine judgement - Adam and Eve, Noah's Ark and Sodom and Gomorrah - all come from the book of Genesis. Yet the theme of God as a judge continues in the Old Testament and is an important theme for the New Testament.

It could be said that one of the big changes between the Jewish tradition of the Old Testament and the Christian tradition of the New Testament is its new emphasis on two things: faith and repentance. In the Ten Commandments, instructions are given for religious practice (what you do), but in the New Testament, it is through faith, through believing in Jesus as the Son of God that you gain eternal life. Part of this faith is true repentance for sins committed, and asking God for forgiveness.

In the New Testament, the image is found of Christ (or the Son of Man as he is called in some passages) sitting in judgement and weighing each person's deeds. This is seen in the Gospel of Matthew in the passage about the "sheep" and the "goats" (the righteous and the unrighteous). The image is of Christ separating them out.

> *31 When the Son of Man comes in his glory, and all the angels with him, he will sit on his glorious throne. 32 All the nations will be gathered before him, and he will separate the people one from another as a shepherd separates the sheep from the goats. 33 He will put the sheep on his right and the goats on his left.*

34 Then the King will say to those on his right, "Come, you who are blessed by my Father; take your inheritance, the kingdom prepared for you since the creation of the world. 35 For I was hungry and you gave me something to eat, I was thirsty and you gave me something to drink, I was a stranger and you invited me in, 36 I needed clothes and you clothed me, I was ill and you looked after me, I was in prison and you came to visit me."

37 Then the righteous will answer him, "Lord, when did we see you hungry and feed you, or thirsty and give you something to drink? 38 When did we see you a stranger and invite you in, or needing clothes and clothe you? 39 When did we see you ill or in prison and go to visit you?"

40 The King will reply, "Truly I tell you, whatever you did for one of the least of these brothers and sisters of mine, you did for me."

41 Then he will say to those on his left, "Depart from me, you who are cursed, into the eternal fire prepared for the devil and his angels. 42 For I was hungry and you gave me nothing to eat, I was thirsty and you gave me nothing to drink, 43 I was a stranger and you did not invite me in, I needed clothes and you did not clothe me, I was ill and in prison and you did not look after me."

44 They also will answer, "Lord, when did we see you hungry or thirsty or a stranger or needing clothes or ill or in prison, and did not help you?"

45 He will reply, "Truly I tell you, whatever you did not do for one of the least of these, you did not do for me."

46 Then they will go away to eternal punishment, but the righteous to eternal life.

(Matthew 25:31-46)

For the faithful; for those who have acted charitably to "the least of these brothers" there is eternal life. For the others, there is eternal punishment.

PROBLEMATIC CASES FOR GOD'S GOODNESS

Reading through some of the narratives in the previous section, we might find some of the examples of divine retribution quite hard to take. In fact there are places, especially in the Old Testament, where we might question whether these are the actions of a good God at all. Here are some instances.

Adam and Eve

WHAT HAPPENS - God commands that Adam and Eve should not eat the fruit of the Tree of the Knowledge of Good and Evil; they break this command and are banished from paradise. They and all their descendants will have to work for their food, and all women will suffer greatly in childbirth.

THE CHALLENGE TO GOD'S GOODNESS - For one action, that presumably an omniscient God would have foreseen anyway, not only are Adam and Eve punished harshly for the duration of their lives, but so are all their descendants. It could be said that God is punishing innocent people for no good reason.

POSSIBLE RESPONSE - Most scholars take the story of the Fall of Man as an allegory for how evil entered the world, rather than a true narrative about actions undertaken by God. The Fall of Man is not so much about God banishing man from paradise, but of Adam and Eve turning away from it, and in a sense, therefore banishing themselves. Moreover, in the Christian tradition it is said that "God so loved the world that He gave His only begotten Son" (John 3:16) to be a sacrifice to atone for all the sins committed by mankind. This act of self-giving re-opens the possibility of entering the Kingdom of Heaven (paradise) to all believers.

This suggests that although the punishment of Adam and Eve is harsh, God does not cut everyone off forever.

BUT STILL ... It is still problematic that God punishes the whole of humanity for one action, and it does not seem just that descendants share in the banishment of humanity.

Abraham and Isaac

WHAT HAPPENS - God commands Abraham to sacrifice his son Isaac, and Abraham obeys, setting out with Isaac to build the altar. God prevents Abraham killing his son, and Abraham sacrifices a ram instead.

THE CHALLENGE TO GOD'S GOODNESS - A good God is commanding Abraham not only to kill another person, but to kill His own son. This seems to be an intrinsically evil thing to command, so not a command of a good God.

POSSIBLE RESPONSE - This narrative is usually interpreted as a test of faith. Abraham's faith in God is unwavering, even when the command is an impossibly hard one to understand. The point is not that God commands this evil action, but that Abraham remains faithful that "God will provide" even in these extreme circumstances.

BUT STILL ... We could question whether an omniscient God should need to test Abraham like this, and even though God does not make Abraham go through with the task, isn't the command itself an evil one? How could a good God even command such a thing?

Noah's Ark

WHAT HAPPENS - God becomes despondent about how evil humanity has become, and regrets making humans in the first place. He decides to send a flood to wipe them from the face of the earth, saving only Noah and his family, along with pairs of animals.

THE CHALLENGE TO GOD'S GOODNESS - It seems problematic that an almighty and omniscient God would regret His actions - how could a God, who knows what will happen, regret something? Surely, God should have known that this would happen? Moreover, it seems that God's first response is to wipe all evil from the face of the earth. He does not attempt to teach the people to be good in the story of Noah's Ark; He simply wipes them out.

POSSIBLE RESPONSE - Despite the fact the punishment seems harsh, we cannot question that this is a story in which God shows righteousness to those who have been wicked, and mercy to those who have been faithful. Would justice be best served by treating Noah in the same way as everyone else? It could also be said that the significance of the story is that God acts to remove the evil in the world.

BUT STILL ... The fact that God's first act is to seemingly massacre everyone apart from Noah's family seems a disproportionate response from a God that is supposed to be good. Moreover, if the meaning of the story of Noah's Ark is that God removes evil from the world, why does He allow atrocities to take place in this day and age?

The story of Job

WHAT HAPPENS - Job is faithful to God and to His law. Satan tries to persuade God that Job is only faithful because of His luck in life; because he has possessions and family. Satan persuades God to let him destroy his possessions, as a test of his faith. Eventually, Satan destroys everything he has, kills his whole family and gives him a disgusting skin disease. After all this, Job questions what he could possibly have done to deserve this, as he has tried so hard to faithfully adhere to the law. God appears "in a storm" and challenges Job, saying "where were you when I beat out the vault of the heavens?", implying that Job is no one to question his creator. Job repents, and eventually God blesses him again. Job has a new family and creates a new life for himself.

THE CHALLENGE TO GOD'S GOODNESS - This is a really difficult story to take. God reproaches Job for questioning Him, but His actions are questionable. The whole reason that God is testing Job is because he is a faithful servant, and yet He tests him to the point of losing almost everything. God is persuaded by Satan to test Job in a way that feels like a bet or a dare; hardly the actions of a good God.

POSSIBLE RESPONSE - The important message of this story could be seen to be that obedience to the law alone is not enough without continuing faith in God, and that without this, obeying the law is empty. It could also be highlighting the idea that the demands of faith are hard, and yet faith is required in all circumstances.

BUT STILL ... The question remains: are the actions that God allows Satan to perform in the story of Job really actions that a good God would permit?

A general response

In general, it could be said that to take these stories as reports of actions that God has perpetrated would be missing the point of these narratives. The point of these storied is not that they tell us what God has said and done, but have religious meanings that we need to extract from them.

Having said this, are religious stories not meant to tell us of the nature of God? Even if these stories are not meant to report events, they portray a God with characteristics that many would struggle to call good.

IS SOMETHING GOOD BECAUSE GOD COMMANDS IT, OR DOES GOD COMMAND IT BECAUSE IT IS GOOD?

In the Euthyphro, Socrates poses the question "Is something pious because it is loved by the gods, or is it loved by the gods because it is pious?" This has since become known as the **EUTHYPHRO DILEMMA**, and although Socrates asks this questions of the gods, it is no less a problem (perhaps more so) for the Judaeo-Christian God.

So, is it God who decides what is good, or does God prescribe the things He knows to be good? There seem to be two possible solutions to this question:

1. Actions become good because God commands them

2. God commands the things He does because they are good.

However, this problem is called a dilemma for a reason: neither solution really seems acceptable. Let's look at the strengths and weaknesses of each solution.

Vision 1

Actions become good because God commands them (known as **DIVINE COMMAND THEORY**).

Support for this view	Problems with this view
God is seen as a law maker, which implies that He decides the law, rather than just tells people what the law is.	*If something is good just because God commands it, then there is nothing inherently good about them. This would mean that they are only good because God says so, not because they are good in and of themselves.*
Abraham is required to obey the command to kill his son Isaac, despite the fact that killing people is generally thought wrong and is later condemned in the Ten Commandments.	
	The implication of this is that God chooses certain things to be right and wrong not because they are right or wrong but because of a whim. Could God's whim change? Could God command that murder was allowed tomorrow, and condemn the eating of candyfloss? If things are only good because God says so, the implication seems to be that He could change His mind.
If God is creator ex nihilo, then it is difficult to explain where good comes from if not from God.	
If God does make something good by commanding it, that makes God an authority; more in keeping with other divine attributes.	

Advocates of Divine Command Theory would say that the idea of a morality that exists separate to God's will makes no sense when you believe in a law-giving God. The most famous advocate of this view is **SØREN KIRKEGAARD,** who thought of Abraham as the epitome of the faithful believer because he was willing to take a "leap of faith". According to Kirkegaard, God's will is what makes something good or bad, so the idea of God commanding something evil is nonsense. God's command is good because of the very fact that God commands it.

Vision 2

God commands things because they are good.

Support for this view	Problems with this view
The behaviour that God tends to condemn in the Bible tends to be behaviour that is harmful, selfish or both. It therefore seems that God is commanding good things, rather than whatever He chooses to command.	*If God does not decide what is good, He is less of a moral authority; He is reduced to a being that proclaims laws rather than invents them.*
This means that God's commands are chosen for good reasons. This fits more with the idea of a benevolent deity.	*Moreover, if God is creator ex nihilo, where did these objective moral standards come from if they are not part of God's creation?*
If God commands what is good, there is no concern that He could change His mind, or command things purely on a whim.	*If God did not create these standards of goodness, then there exists something in His creation over which He has no control. If these standards are outside His control, does that mean He is also subject to these laws?*
If God is commanding things because they are intrinsically good, then God seems more justified in punishing those that do not meet these standards. Otherwise, it seems that He is punishing those who are not living according to the standards He happens to have set.	*Not only would this diminish His role as law giver, but it would also reduce Him to being a judge of whether people live up to external standards, rather than His own.*

Neither solution seems to be adequate. On the one hand, we have a God setting standards without those standards being intrinsically good, and on the other hand we have a God who has no control over goodness.

A middle way?

AQUINAS, and much more recently **WILLIAM LANE CRAIG**, proposed a third solution to the Euthyphro Dilemma. According to their view, God does not command things because they are good, and things do not become good through God commanding them. Instead, God commands things because **HE IS GOOD**. We can see immediately how this might cohere with the idea of God's goodness as being ultimate perfection or the highest good. If God is ultimate goodness, then it follows that anything He commands will be intrinsically good. This solution allows for God to be the ultimate moral authority without losing a sense of the intrinsic goodness of the commands God makes.

CAN A GOOD GOD REWARD AND PUNISH?

If you have any interest in the medieval period at all - even perhaps if you do not - you will have come across those amazing paintings and carvings depicting visions of Hell. In these, you see people being tortured on racks, being eaten by enormous monsters, along with numerous other punishments, all within a context of fiery torment.

The question this poses for us is whether a good God could allow this to happen. Could a benevolent God raise some people heavenwards, and condemn others to Hell? Is an eternity of torture something that a good God could send His creatures to?

Biblical evidence

Looking back to the theme of God as a judge earlier in this chapter, we can see that there is New Testament evidence that the "Son of Man" will condemn the "eternal punishment" and reward the righteous with "eternal life".

In the Book of Revelation, the only book of prophesy in the New Testament, which foretells the end of the world, we hear an even harsher reality of judgement:

> *11 Then I saw a great white throne and him who was seated on it. The earth and the heavens fled from his presence, and there was no place for them. 12 And I saw the dead, great and small, standing before the throne, and books were opened. Another book was opened, which is the book of life. The dead were judged according to what they had done as recorded in the books. 13 The sea gave up the*

*dead that were in it, and death and Hades gave up the dead that were
in them, and each person was judged according to what they had
done. 14 Then death and Hades were thrown into the lake of fire. The
lake of fire is the second death. 15 Anyone whose name was not found
written in the book of life was thrown into the lake of fire. (Revelation
20:11-15)*

It seems clear that there is a message in the Bible about rewards and
punishment, and that therefore God does allow these things. What
remains is to examine whether a good God would allow these things.

WILLIAM LANE CRAIG believes that Hell is required as a
manifestation of God's goodness. If God "blinked at sin" - if He ignored
it - then He would be unjust, and an unjust God is not a good God. If
there are no punishments that result from rejecting God, then there is no
differentiation made between those who accept and those who reject
God. Lane Craig argues that God's goodness requires that that does not
happen.

However, Lane Craig does not see Hell as being like the depictions we
see in medieval art or in Dante's Inferno. He thinks that God's goodness
requires Hell, but not a Hell of that nature. Instead, He thinks of Hell as
how it is depicted in 2 Thessalonians 1:9, where Paul describes it as
"exclusion from the presence of God". Lane Craig interprets Hell as a
rejection of God in our life. Hell therefore becomes an existence where
we are trapped by our selfish wants, fears and desires, with no hope of
the presence of God; effectively Lane Craig sees Hell as being trapped in
our own egos.

JOHN HICK takes a different view. In his book Evil and the God of Love, he advances the view that God allows evil in the world in order to develop our souls to spiritual maturity. This testing and gradual development means that Hick hopes "that God will eventually succeed in His purpose of winning all men to Himself in faith and love". (Evil and the God of Love p. 342)

Evil on Earth is a way of developing souls to spiritual maturity, and this in Hick's view would replace the need for punitive evil taking place in Hell. As people at the end of their lives might not have reached spiritual maturity, Hick posits what he calls an "intermediate state", which allows the time for souls to develop into a likeness of God, enabling them to be part of the Kingdom of Heaven. Hick suggests that Hell does not need to be a reality with God, because given enough time for souls to develop, eventually everyone becomes worthy of the Kingdom of Heaven. A God of Love would not want to reject a single part of His creation, and this view hopes that He would not need to.

KEITH WARD, in his book Re-thinking Christianity, poses a problem to the kind of view that Hick espouses. Ward believes that it is always "possible for rational creatures to exclude themselves from love", (p. 42) and so it is always possible for a free agent to choose not to accept God. This is a common idea in Christian thinking, that a good God allows us to freely choose whether to accept Him or not, so the possibility that some will exclude themselves from God must always be there.

Ward notes that the depiction of Hell in the New Testament (that we examined above) seems not to fully comprehend the significance of the crucifixion. He believes that "[t]he true Christian perception is that the cross of Christ is God's last word on violence. The divine love will never turn into divine hatred. It will go as far as possible to bring people to divine life, and it will always seek the welfare of every sentient being.

And that is the last word." (p. 42) Like William Lane Craig, Ward therefore sees Hell as not a state of torture and violence but a wilful exclusion of oneself from the love of God.

Importantly, Ward thinks that God does everything He can to call those who reject Him back to His love. Ward quotes the Gospel of Luke, where Jesus says that "I came not to call the righteous, but sinners, to repentance." (Luke 5:32) Ward therefore thinks that God goes as far as He can to bring people back to Him and save them from exclusion from His love, but there must always be the possibility to reject Him; God gave His creatures freedom to do so. Interestingly, therefore, God does not condemn people to Hell; people make that choice for themselves. What God does, according to Ward, is leave that possibility open because human beings are free.

CONCLUSION

A point of similarity between these scholars is that God does not torture or punish in Hell; a good God does not allow that. But for those, like William Lane Craig and Keith Ward, who believe Hell has to be possible, it is seen as a separation from the love of God rather than a torment to which God condemns people.

FURTHER READING

Davies, B An Introduction to The Philosophy of Religion, OUP, 2004, Ch. 12

GOLDBERG, D & RAYNER, J The Jewish People: Their History and Their Religion, Penguin, 1989, Chs. 1 & 2

VARDY, P & ARLISS J The Thinker's Guide to God, John Hunt Publishing, 2004, Ch. 7

Omnipotence

KEY TERMS

ALMIGHTY - The most powerful thing. A being that is the most powerful thing but is not necessarily able to do everything.

IN CONFLICT WITH GOD'S NATURE - Something that is not impossible, but conflicts with another aspect of God's nature.

LOGICALLY IMPOSSIBLE - Something impossible given the laws of logic as they are (eg $2 + 2 = 5$).

OMNIPOTENT - All-powerful. Can do anything, or according to Augustine, "what He wills".

PHYSICALLY IMPOSSIBLE - Something impossible given the laws of nature as they are (eg lead floating).

PSEUDO TASKS - Aquinas's term for things that seem, grammatically, like tasks, but are not because they are intrinsically impossible; not something that can be done.

We said earlier (see table at the end of the Introduction) that the idea of God's power is apparent in the Bible, but that the idea of God as an omnipotent being is one that comes about through Church tradition, rather than being directly claimed in scripture. There is much evidence of God's great power (we only have to think of events such as the Parting of the Red Sea to be reminded of this), but there is relatively little evidence that the God of Sacred Scripture is omnipotent.

Perhaps the best example from scripture to support a claim of God's omnipotence is found in the Gospel of Luke in the story of the Annunciation, where the Angel Gabriel tells Mary that her cousin Elizabeth, thought to be infertile, was going to have a baby. Gabriel says that "nothing is impossible with God". (Luke 1:37) This seems to suggest that God is omnipotent because nothing is impossible for him to do. However, some translations say something quite different. The New International Version says "no word from God will ever fail". Whereas the first translation suggests God's omnipotence, this translation does not; it simply claims that God's actions do not fail. We can see that there is scant evidence at best for God's omnipotence in the Bible.

So, where does this idea of God's omnipotence originate?

By the time of the writing of the Nicene Creed, in 325 CE, God was described as "Pater omnipotens", but **VARDY** argues that this is best translated as "father almighty" rather than "omnipotent father". The word "almighty" implies that God is the most powerful being, but it does not imply a being that can do anything. Certainly, when the Nicene Creed is pronounced in churches today, the translation most often used is:

I believe in God
The Father almighty
Maker of Heaven and Earth.

So, although the Creed of 325 CE (in its Latin translation) calls God "omnipotens", this does not necessarily mean that it is being claimed that God is omnipotent.

In the 5th C, **AUGUSTINE**, in his book City of God, claims that God "is called omnipotent on account of His doing what He wills". (Book V.x) This claims that God's power is more than simply "the most powerful being"; this is a claim that God can do all He wants; this is a claim of omnipotence.

The idea of God as an omnipotent being is therefore present at least from the time of Augustine. Omnipotence may not be explicitly biblical, but it does date back to early Christian thinking.

So, according to Augustine, God can do what he wants to do. Others have defined omnipotence literally as "all powerful"; able to do anything. Does this imply that God can perform these tasks?

1. Can God sin?

2. Can God change the past?

3. Can God commit suicide?

4. Can God make $2 + 2 = 5$?

5. Can God make water boil at 20C?

Each of these actions would seem on the face of it to be problematic.

- If God can commit a sin, then this compromises His omnibenevolence, His goodness; so God being able to sin conflicts with one of His other attributes. If God truly is omnipotent, it seems that He should be able to sin; it seems odd if He is constrained from doing something that humans do all the time. At the same time, though, the idea of an omnibenevolent God seems to require that He never sins, otherwise He would not be all good. Therefore, it seems that He **MUST** be able to sin in order to be omnipotent, and **MUST NOT** be able to sin in order to be omnibenevolent.

- Changing the past seems difficult because we would normally hold the past to be fixed. The present and future might be yet determinable, but the past seems set in stone. Could God make it such that Elizabeth I had children? That would change a huge amount about the future. Maybe the crowns of England and Scotland would have never joined, and Great Britain would have never been formed? If the Stuarts did not come to power, then the Civil War, the regicide of Charles I, the Commonwealth and the Restoration would perhaps not have happened. Does God's omnipotence mean that He ought to be able to fiddle with all these things? This question also relates to discussions about God's relationship with time, because if God is everlasting, but in time, He would be acting now to change the past, which would involve what philosophers call **BACKWARDS CAUSATION**; a cause cannot happen after its effect. Having said this, if God is outside time altogether, perhaps His changing the past is less of a problem.

- God committing suicide seems problematic for three reasons. First, the Church traditionally holds suicide to be a sin, so as we said above, that would compromise His goodness. Second, God is held to be the sustainer of the world: He both created the world and keeps it in existence. Were God to commit suicide, the universe would simultaneously be destroyed. Third, God is held by many to not be a being, but **BEING ITSELF**, and so you could say it is incoherent for something whose essence is being to not-be.

- For God to make $2 + 2 = 5$, the laws of mathematics would have to be overturned, and there is an interesting debate about whether God could do this. If God created the laws of logic and mathematics, then perhaps He could break them, or they could, in some way, not apply to Him. On the other hand, it seems senseless to say that God could have two sets of two things and yet there be five things. This issue will provide interesting subject matter for discussion later on.

- For God to make water boil at 20C, He would have to undermine the laws of nature. Now, as creator of the world, the laws of nature are part of His invention, and so perhaps He is above the laws of nature, but He would have to change the properties of water completely for water to boil at 20C. Moreover, were He to do this, our blood would boil, which might conflict with His attribute of goodness ...

These actions seem problematic, then, for a number of different kinds of reasons. Either, they seem like tasks that could be **INTRINSICALLY IMPOSSIBLE** (like making $2 + 2 = 5$, or changing the past) or which **CONFLICT WITH HIS NATURE** (like sinning or committing suicide).

If God is truly omnipotent, then it seems to follow perhaps that He should be able to do anything, including these problematic actions. If God cannot do these things, does that mean He cannot be called omnipotent?

A PROBLEMATIC ROCK

A number of puzzles have been created by philosophers to test the concept of omnipotence. A particularly memorable puzzle is as follows:

Can God create a rock that is so large that He cannot lift it?

This is of course a paradox: a problem where any solution is unacceptable. If God can create the rock, then He cannot lift it. The other option, on the other hand, is that he cannot make the rock. Either solution entails something that God cannot do. Perhaps this paradox shows us that the idea of omnipotence is not cogent.

THREE APPROACHES TO OMNIPOTENCE

There are three ways of approaching omnipotence, and these problematic actions:

1. Deny God's omnipotence.

2. Claim that an omnipotent God can do absolutely anything, irrespective of whether it seems logical that He should do so.

3. Claim that omnipotence does not entail that God should be able to do absolutely anything.

Option 1 - process theology

Our first option is the most modern. Process theology is an outlook on the nature of God that was initiated by the work of Whitehead (1861-1947), and later Hartshorne (1897-2000). The claim of process theology is that God's nature is different to how it is normally conceived. God, as conceived by process theology, is not omnipotent in the sense of being able to do anything. God can persuade, but cannot force; some things are, therefore out of God's control. Moreover, in an act of self-limiting, God is able to be affected by creation; the world can change Him. Process theologians see God as in time, and affected by time.

According to process theology, there are plenty of actions that God cannot perform. Therefore, the actions that we listed above would provide no difficulty for this view, as process theologians reject the traditional idea of omnipotence.

Evaluation of process theology

In one sense, this view solves the problem by denying that there is a problem. By saying that God's power does not entail that He should be able to do absolutely anything, and indeed claiming that there are many things God cannot do, the actions that we listed no longer pose a problem. Simply put, if God cannot do everything anyway, then these particular examples do not challenge a concept of God's power.

However, process theology is quite controversial because it denies many things that are held to be central to God's nature as Christianity conceives of it. If there are many things that God cannot do; if indeed God can be affected by the world, what real meaning is there in saying that God is omnipotent? Rather than being all-powerful, this envisaging of God seems rather lacking in power.

Option 2 - Descartes

Descartes' solution to problems with God's omnipotence is quite the reverse of process theology. Descartes claims that God, as omnipotent and creator of the world, can do anything, even if, to us, it seems incoherent that He should do so.

Descartes argued that as God created the world, He set up the laws of nature and logic. He would, therefore, not be subject to these laws, as He made them.

The idea of God making $2 + 2 = 5$ may seem utterly impossible to us: if there are two things, and you add another two things, you cannot make five things however hard you try, even if you are God. However, Descartes argues that we think that this is impossible, not because God's power has limits, but because our minds do. If you have studied anything of Descartes' thought, you will know that his most celebrated contribution to Philosophy is his use of scepticism (doubt) to enquire into what we can really know for certain. In his book The Meditations, Descartes says that we cannot be certain that what we perceive really is the case; after all we could be dreaming. Even our beliefs about mathematical truths could be wrong. After all, we have all made mistakes in maths at some time: how can we know for certain we have not made an error? According to Descartes, everything we hold to be true can, in theory, be doubted. Now if none of our beliefs including those about logic and mathematics is indubitable, it follows that although it might to us seem inconceivable that $2 + 2 = 5$, that does not mean that it definitely could not be the case; we could be wrong.

So, according to Descartes, however impossible something might seem to us, that reflects only the limits of our intelligence, rather than the limits of God's power.

Evaluation of Descartes' view

Intuitively, Descartes' view might seem more palatable than that of process theologians, who deny many of the attributes that we might consider central to the nature of God. According to Descartes, God is omnipotent in an extremely strong sense: He really can do anything - even things that seem inconceivable to us. Descartes prompts us to ask ourselves: which is more likely, that God cannot perform certain actions or that humans cannot conceive of everything that God does? As the old hymn says: "God moves in a mysterious way, His wonders to perform."

However, there are considerable difficulties with this view. First of all, do we really believe that $2 + 2$ cannot equal 5 because it is inconceivable to us, or because it is not cogent that two sets of two things could ever equal 5? Take another example: can God make a circular square? A square, if it were circular, would not fit the definition of a square; a circle with four sides of equal length and four corners of 90 degrees could not be a circle. Our denial that God could make such a shape, or make 2 + 2 = 5, has nothing to do with the limits of our minds, but the limits of possibility. A square circle is not a circle, and four things cannot be five things, so it could be argued that the idea of God doing these things is, as **KENNY** said in his book on Aquinas, utter nonsense.

Secondly, even if you admit that God ought to be able to perform these kinds of task, Descartes has paid no attention to tasks that might undermine His nature: he has failed to address the question of whether God could sin, or commit suicide. His view is that there is nothing God cannot do, yet Descartes himself defined God as a perfect being; which would suggest that He cannot sin. This is an important area that Descartes failed to tackle.

Option 3 - Aquinas

So we come to our third option. Aquinas's view is a middle way between on the one hand, process theologians, who deny that God is omnipotent in the normal sense, and on the other hand Descartes, who believes that God can perform even actions that seem nonsensical.

Aquinas claims that omnipotence does not have to entail performing absolutely any task. There are two sorts of actions that Aquinas believes are not required of an omnipotent God.

1. Actions that grammatically seem like tasks, but which are nonsense. Aquinas said that tasks like creating an unliftable

rock, making $2 + 2 = 5$ or creating a square circle seem on the face of it to be tasks. Grammatically, we can add the words "Can God ... ?" and it seems as though we are asking whether this is a task that God can perform. However, according to Aquinas, just because grammatically it sounds as though we are talking about a task, in fact, these actions are not cogent; they are utter nonsense. Aquinas posits then that there is no problem at all if God cannot perform these tasks, because it is inconceivable that any being could. In fact, these are not tasks, they are **PSEUDO TASKS**.

2. Actions that go against the nature of God. Aquinas said that an omnipotent God was not less powerful if He could not do things that conflict with His nature. Aquinas would say that God could neither sin nor commit suicide, because these actions would be against His nature. Nothing is lost, claims Aquinas, if God cannot compromise His other attributes. After all, why would we want a God that could sin? Nothing of the nature of God is diminished if this is something that He cannot do.

Evaluation of Aquinas

Aquinas's solution seems to solve the problems of both process theology and Descartes' solutions by maintaining a strong notion of the omnipotence of God without claiming that He must be able to perform impossible tasks or act against His nature. This middle way gives us a notion of omnipotence that demands exactly enough of God's power.

However, supporters of Descartes' view might suggest that Aquinas's view of God is extremely powerful, but strictly not omnipotent, because there are things He cannot do. As **VARDY** suggests, perhaps Aquinas is actually defending the idea of an almighty God, not strictly an omnipotent one.

This depends, though on how we define omnipotence. If we go back to Augustine's definition, that God "is called omnipotent on account of His doing what He wills", there is no problem, as God, as omnibenevolent sustainer of the universe, would not want to sin or commit suicide. Aquinas's view allows that God can do any task that falls within Augustine's definition.

CONCLUSION

Aquinas's response in the debate about omnipotence has become the generally accepted view amongst many theologians and philosophers, but it is true that this is not a God that could do absolutely anything. It can be meaningfully argued that strictly, only Descartes' solution allows for this, but if we deny that God can perform nonsense tasks like making a square circle, and tasks that go against His nature, like sinning, it hardly seems as though His omnipotence has been compromised in a way that is significant.

FURTHER READING

CLACK, B & CLACK, BR The Philosophy of Religion: A Critical Introduction, Polity Press, 2008, Ch. 2 section II

DAVIES, B An Introduction to The Philosophy of Religion, OUP, 2004, Ch. 9

VARDY, P & ARLISS J The Thinker's Guide to God, John Hunt Publishing, 2004, Ch. 7

Omniscience

KEY WORDS

BEING ACQUAINTED WITH - Knowledge of people or things; a different kind of knowledge.

FOREKNOWLEDGE - Knowledge of the future.

KNOWING THAT - Knowledge of facts. What philosophers would call "propositional knowledge".

MIDDLE KNOWLEDGE - Molina's view that God knows how possible created beings would act in certain circumstances.

ONTOLOGICAL PROBLEM - The problem that God cannot know the future because there is no future to know.

PROBLEM OF FREEDOM - The problem that God cannot know the future because if He did, our freedom would be compromised.

Of all the terms so often used of God, such as being omnipotent, omnipresent and omnibenevolent, the idea of God being omniscient is in some ways the least controversial. The Bible never directly claims that God is all-powerful, but that His power is great; it says He is good, but events such as the Flood might provoke us to question what precisely is meant by God's goodness. It is only in the case of omniscience that the concepts of God in classical theism and in the Bible seem to map on to each other perfectly: both hold Him to be omniscient.

In Isaiah, we hear that "my thoughts are not your thoughts ...", (Is. 55:8) which makes clear how different the divine mind is. God's knowledge is not like our knowledge; perhaps the difference between them is that God's knowledge is unlimited. As we hear in 1 John 3:20, "If our hearts condemn us, we know that God is greater than our hearts, and he knows everything." Interestingly, it is a question of knowledge that lies at the centre of the narrative of the Garden of Eden: Adam and Eve eat the fruit from the tree of the **KNOWLEDGE OF GOOD AND EVIL**. The first exercise of human freedom comes in wanting to know what God knows, and throughout the Bible, a wonder at God's knowledge prevails, as we see in Psalm 139:2, where it says that God knows "when I sit and when I rise; you perceive my thoughts from afar".

CLACK AND CLACK make it clear why God's omniscience is so uncontroversial by quoting **THOMAS MORRIS**:

> If knowledge is an intrinsic good, then the property of being knowledgeable is a great-making property. And if the value of knowledge is additive ("the more the better"), then to have total knowledge is greater than to have incomplete knowledge. - Morris, Our Idea of God, p. 83

Knowledge is a perfection, so it follows that the more knowledge God has, the better. It is therefore a reasonable thing to claim that the being that Anselm called "that than which no greater can be conceived" must know everything, because it is greatest to know everything there is to know. The question for us then is not whether God is omniscient, but what omniscience entails.

TYPES OF KNOWLEDGE

English is, in many ways, an impoverished language when it comes to talking of knowledge, because we use the same verb "to know" for so many different kinds of thing. Look at the following instances of knowledge:

1. Bert knows that Croydon is south of London.

2. Bert knows Brian.

3. Bert knows how to ride a bike.

Here, Bert has three kinds of knowledge that in other languages would be expressed using different verbs. In French and German, and doubtless many other languages, there are two different verbs for **KNOWING THAT** and **BEING ACQUAINTED WITH**. In French, knowing that x uses the verb savoir (from which we get our word "savvy"); in German, knowing that x uses the word wissen, which has the same root as our words "wise" and "wisdom". So Brian's knowledge that Croydon is south of London is knowledge of a fact; the kind of knowledge for which savoir and wissen are used.

On the other hand, Bert knowing Brian is not knowledge of a fact; it is an acquaintance with something, or in this case, someone. We would still use the same old verb "to know", but in French they would use connaître (which has the same root as our word "connect"), and in German, they would use kennen (related to ken in Scots). Bert knowing Brian is a different kind of knowledge to his knowledge that Croydon is south of London. Bert might know facts about Brian, like whether or not he has glasses, but that is not the same as acquaintance with him - to know Brian is to know something more than just facts about him.

Bert knowing how to ride a bike is another kind of knowledge again: know-how; the possession of a skill. When we say that Bert knows how to ride a bike, we mean that he knows how to do the things necessary to be riding a bike; in other words, he can ride a bike.

So, if we look back at the examples, we see that there are three kinds of knowledge:

- **KNOWLEDGE-THAT** (Croydon is south of London)

- **ACQUAINTANCE WITH** (Bert knows Brian)

- **KNOW-HOW** (riding a bike)

WHAT DOES GOD KNOW?

We have said that God is omniscient (all-knowing), but now we know that there are three kinds of knowledge, does God's omniscience entail having all these?

Knowledge-that

God uncontroversially knows all facts there are to know. As it says in Job: "To God belong wisdom and power; counsel and understanding are his". As creator of the world, especially if He created ex nihilo, it follows that God knows everything about His creation, and that His knowledge of all the facts about the world would be complete.

Acquaintance with

It is also uncontroversial that God has an intimate acquaintance with His creation; this is at the heart of the theistic way of conceiving of God, as opposed to a deist understanding of Him. Unlike Aristotle's Prime Mover, the Judaeo-Christian God is one involved with the world, not indifferent to it. As it says in Luke 16:15, "God knows your hearts". Traditionally, Christians would claim that God's acquaintance with us is closer than any other relationship, and humans reaching out to have a relationship with God is central to religious practice.

Know-how

This is the most controversial kind of knowledge for God to possess. We have said that know-how implies a skill: the know-how to ride a bike is the skill required to ride a bike. However, it seems that know-how is something God must not have in many cases. God cannot, for example, ride a bike because He is incorporeal; He has no legs. Similarly, He cannot have the know-how to brush His teeth or tie His shoelaces, because these are not the actions of a being with no body. It seems that God does not have the know-how that humans have. Still, that does not mean that He could not have a complete factual knowledge (knowledge that) of everything humans need to acquire know-how. God could know precisely what needs to be done to drive a car effectively and safely, without having the know-how to drive a car Himself.

FOREKNOWLEDGE

The most problematic question for God's knowledge comes when we ask whether God can know the future. It seems that if God knows everything, then God should know the future. Moreover, there is a long biblical tradition (both in the Old Testament and, to a lesser extent, in the New Testament) of prophesy; of God speaking through prophets about what will happen.

There are two problems associated with God foreknowing (knowing the future), which I will call the ontological problem and the problem of freedom. An account that deals convincingly with the problem of God's divine foreknowledge will provide answers to both of these problems.

THE ONTOLOGICAL PROBLEM is a problem with the future fact that is said to be known. It is an ontological problem because it is to do with the existence (which in Greek is ontos) of the future state of affairs. Take the proposition "Clare is typing". This is a claim about a present state of affairs - that Clare is doing something now, namely typing. This proposition is either true or false, because I am either typing or I'm not. But what about the proposition "Clare will type tomorrow"? This does not seem to be a proposition of the same kind, because it seems there is no fact yet to which this claim can relate. It is not yet true that I will, because tomorrow isn't here yet, but at the same time, the proposition is not false either, because I might type tomorrow - "Clare will type tomorrow" is not definitely false. Many philosophers would say that the future is not yet determined - there are no facts about tomorrow yet.

IMAGINE THE CLAIM IS ...	THE STATE OF AFFAIRS MIGHT BE ...	IN THIS CASE, THE CLAIM WOULD THEREFORE BE ...
Clare is typing	*There is someone called Clare who is typing*	*TRUE*
Clare is typing	*There is no one called Clare who is typing*	*FALSE*
Clare will type tomorrow	*???? - the future is not determined - there are no future states of affairs to which this relates*	*Indeterminate - neither true nor false*

So, in brief, the ontological problem with foreknowledge is this: It seems that claims about the future cannot be true or false, hence they cannot be known because you can only know something that is true.

THE PROBLEM OF FREEDOM follows on from the ontological problem. If you believe that God knows the future, then it seems that you have to say that the future is not as indeterminate as it seems to be (not true or false yet), but that it is fixed, and there are facts about the future that are true or false. Now if we conclude that the future must be fixed, (as God knows it), then it seems that our free will is a nonsense, because if God knows what we are going to do tomorrow, then we cannot do otherwise; hence we are not free to choose today what we will do tomorrow.

The problem of freedom briefly is this: If God knows the future, there is a future to know, and hence I do not bring my future to be through free choice, but rather it is fixed and unchangeable.

SOLUTIONS TO THE PROBLEM OF FOREKNOWLEDGE

There have been many attempts to sufficiently respond to this problem, stretching back to very early Christian writers, and continuing to this day.

1. God knows what someone would choose in certain circumstances

The first option we will examine is presented to us by the Jesuit thinker **MOLINA** (1536-1600). He says that God's knowledge is not simply of the future, but of "what would happen if ..." Molina calls this God's **MIDDLE KNOWLEDGE** (scientia media). Molina claims that God knows what would happen when theoretically possible people freely acted, and so having created some free-acting people, God knows what will happen, through his middle knowledge of how their choices will play out.

So, imagine God conceives of a possible created being, and conceives that this being will wear a blue suit on Tuesday, given that she is planning to do something on Tuesday that requires wearing a suit, and given that she forgot to pick up her other suit from the dry-cleaners on Monday. God knows what she will wear on Tuesday, because He has a middle knowledge of how she will choose given what circumstances she finds herself in. Molina's envisaging of divine foreknowledge is not one that endangers free will, but one that is more akin to the omniscience of an author, who imaginatively conceives of how certain characters would behave in the circumstances with which they are presented.

Strengths of Molina's view

Undoubtedly, this view goes some way towards solving both problems to do with foreknowledge. It could be said that this overcomes the ontological problem by saying that God does not know future facts, but what modern philosophers would call **COUNTERFACTUALS**, which are statements of possibility. God does not know that x will happen in the future per se, but that were there to be a created being such as this, they would choose in this way at this time in this set of circumstances. God having created this being, He can say they will choose in this way.

Middle knowledge also goes some way towards responding to the problem of freedom, as it is clear that at the centre of Molina's view is the idea of God conceiving of freely acting beings - God knows what His creatures will choose; He does not set out the future or determine that they will act in a certain way. It seems at first that Molina has preserved both God's foreknowledge and human freedom.

Criticisms of middle knowledge

Central to Molina's view is the idea that God conceives of free creatures, and knows what their choices would be, thus not controlling their actions. However, if we go back to our analogy of the omniscient author, we can see how problematic Molina's idea is. The author creates characters and imagines how these characters will act given the circumstances in the novel. How different is this really to determining that a character acts in such-and-such a way? Many authors might say that they create characters and try to imaginatively enter into the way in which that character might behave in certain circumstances, but fundamentally, they are creating both the character and with it, the choices the character will make. If God, as Molina says He does, conceived of possible uncreated beings, and knows how their choices will pan out, are we not bound by the imaginings of our author, as are the characters in the book?

There is an even bigger challenge than this to Molina's view, though. God's middle knowledge is of what a given creature would do in certain circumstances. His knowledge is of the form "if x, then y", where x is the circumstance, and y is the choice. He knows what the value of y is, whatever circumstance x is. But as **BRIAN DAVIES** notes, this seems to lead to absurdity. Davies gives the example of someone who dies as a child. Presumably, God would have to know what that child would have chosen had they not died when they did (ie in a different set of circumstances). But this seems strange, to say the least, because any claim about what that child did when she grew up would surely be false. Yet if we take Molina's view to its logical conclusion, it seems as though God ought to know it anyway. This is an untenable view; you cannot know something that is false. Molina's view is on rocky ground.

2. Knowing does not imply deciding

The second argument is an old one, but one that is associated nowadays with **WILLIAM LANE CRAIG**, a philosopher who often reiterates, simplifies or explains well-established views on religion from philosophers and theologians, as well as offering his own responses.

Lane Craig argues that God's knowledge of the future does not imply His control of it, and hence God can know what will happen whilst it remains a freely chosen event. We can see that knowledge and control are different by looking at an example: I know there is a traffic warden outside my window, but I did not put him there; I have no control over the traffic warden's movements, and my knowing that he's there does not give me any control over him. Lane Craig says that we make a mistake about God's knowledge of the future because we cannot know it. If God knows it and we do not, it makes us feel as though He defines what it will be. This is, however, in Lane Craig's view, confused.

God foreknowing that I will do x, according to Lane Craig, is dependent on my doing x, and my doing x is dependent on my choosing to do x. The problem of God's foreknowledge states that since God foreknows I will do x, I have to do x. Lane Craig's solution is that God can only foreknow x because you will choose to do x, and if you did not choose to do x, God would not foreknow it.

William Lane Craig uses the example of lawnmowing to explain his point:

> The reason God foreknows that Jones will mow his lawn is the simple fact that Jones will mow his lawn. Jones is free to refrain, and were he to do so, God would have foreknown that he would refrain. Jones is free to do whatever he wants, and God's foreknowledge logically follows Jones' action like a shadow, even if chronologically the shadow precedes the coming of the event itself. William Lane Craig, The Only Wise God, p. 74

Strengths of Lane Craig's view

Lane Craig has demonstrated effectively the disconnect between knowing x and being the person who decided x; he has shown that to know x does not imply having any control over x. He has also established firmly the connection between God's knowledge and the facts by arguing that God foreknows x because x will happen, not because God decides it will happen. Many might argue that Lane Craig has effectively diffused the problem of freedom.

Criticisms

Lane Craig offers an appealing response to the problem of freedom, but he has failed to address the other problem with God's foreknowledge. The ontological problem states that it seems God cannot know the future because there is no future to know. Lane Craig has offered no solution to this problem whatsoever.

More than this, his solution to the problem of freedom propels us right back to the ontological problem. In his example of Jones mowing the lawn, he says that "God's foreknowledge logically follows Jones' action like a shadow, even if chronologically the shadow precedes the coming of the event itself". This seems deeply problematic. How can a shadow pre-exist the object that creates it? How could God possibly foreknow an object of knowledge (a state of affairs) that does not yet exist?

Lane Craig may have offered a solution to the problem of freedom, but fails to address the ontological problem; his conception of foreknowledge seems in fact to make it worse.

3. God does not know the future, but knows timelessly what we perceive as future

The final solution we will examine was formulated by **BOETHIUS** in reply to the kind of view that Lane Craig espouses. Boethius is an extremely important figure in Philosophy in a time of great transition. He was born in the middle of the 5th C, and so was alive a century after the

Sack of Rome. The Roman Empire occupied two centres - one in the East at Constantinople, and one in the West at Ravenna. Italy, where Boethius lived, was ruled by the Ostrogoth King Theodoric; Romans and Ostrogoths (a tribe that had been part of the invasion of Rome) lived side by side. Both Romans and Ostrogoths were Christians, but the Ostrogoths did not accept that Christ was fully divine, which led to theological disputes. In his 40s, Boethius became chief minister to Theodoric, which seems to have sealed his fate: he fell out of favour with Theodoric, was imprisoned and was put to death. Some say he was cut down by swords in front of Theodoric's judgement seat; others say he was clubbed to death.

His early death did not affect his significance to philosophy, and he became an important source on which future philosophers would draw. Amongst these, the most notable perhaps from our perspective is Aquinas, but it is important to note that Boethius had an influence in Jewish and Islamic thinking as well as Christian theology. His ideas about foreknowledge form the final book of his Consolation of Philosophy, a dialogue between Boethius and a personification of Philosophy, written very shortly before his death.

Boethius highlights the two problems with God's foreknowledge noted above. He said that "if anything is about to be, and yet its occurrence is not certain and necessary, how can anyone foreknow that it will occur?" (Consolation of Philosophy V.iii) This is what we have been calling the ontological problem. He also recognises the problem of freedom, claiming that if God foreknows what will happen, "vainly are rewards and punishments proposed for the good and bad ... nothing is left free to human design". (ibid.) It is both of these problems that Boethius intends to address.

Boethius is also concerned with an additional problem entailed by the problem of freedom: that if God's foreknowledge means we are not free, then morality and punishment become a nonsense; they both require free will. This point is perhaps best explained in Boethius's own words:

> Vainly are rewards and punishments proposed for the good and bad, since no free and voluntary motion of the will has deserved either one or the other; nay, the punishment of the wicked and the reward of the righteous, which is now esteemed the perfection of justice, will seem the most flagrant injustice, since men are determined either way not by their own proper volition, but by the necessity of what must surely be. And therefore neither virtue nor vice is anything, but rather good and ill desert are confounded together without distinction. - Boethius, Consolation of Philosophy, V.iii

Boethius is therefore trying to find a solution to three strands:

1. The fact that the future is not fixed, so it is hard to see how it could be known at all.

2. If God does know the future, the danger seems to be that we have no freedom.

3. If we have no freedom, there is no vice or virtue, and any punishment God gives is unjust.

Boethius's breakthrough comes when he considers the way in which we know things. Knowledge is influenced not only by the nature of the event, but also by the nature of the knower. If I were colour-blind, I would be unable to know the world in the same way as someone with full-colour vision. So foreknowledge is not simply a problem that calls

117

into question the nature of the event (whether it is fixed; whether it can be changed; whether it is freely chosen) but also the nature of the knower.

Foreknowledge is the preserve of God - humans do not know the future, and so we need to think about what foreknowledge is when we consider the nature of its knower (namely, God). Now, God is eternal, and by that, Boethius means not simply an unending life, but one that is in a certain sense outside of time (see the chapter on eternity). God is eternal, and hence his knowledge is also eternal. It follows, therefore, that God cannot foreknow anything, because foreknowing means "knowing before" and God is not in time. Boethius argues that God cannot know temporally, but knows everything from His standpoint of eternity. Boethius therefore claims that God knows what we would call the future by denying that it is future to Him.

Aquinas's view on divine foreknowledge was influenced heavily by Boethius. He too believed that God knows from a standpoint of eternity, and used the example of a watchtower to illustrate his view.

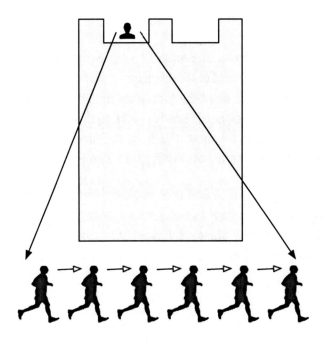

Imagine a watchtower with someone standing at the top, looking out at the world below. In front of the tower is passing a procession of people. Each person in the procession can only see the person ahead of him, but the person at the top of the watchtower can see everything at once.

This is, Aquinas claims, like God's knowledge. We are like the people in the procession, only seeing what is just ahead of us. God is like the man at the top of the watchtower, seeing everything. He sees from His perspective of eternity and hence takes everything in. To the God's eye view, nothing is past, present or future, but is viewed as a whole.

Strengths of Boethius's view

One of the key strengths of Boethius's view is that it draws on other attributes of God than that of His omniscience alone. By appealing to His eternity, as well as His simplicity (not being composed of parts) and His immutability (changelessness), Boethius and Aquinas hold a view about God's knowledge that is coherent with the theistic conception of God as a whole. It ties in with other attributes God is said to have.

In addition, by saying that God does not know temporally but eternally, they avoid absurdities such as God knowing a state of affairs that does not exist yet - this view offers a solution both to the ontological problem of God's foreknowledge as well as the problem of freedom.

Criticisms

Having said this, William Lane Craig would argue that this kind of solution is less successful than it appears. He claims that Aquinas and Boethius seem to hold an **A-THEORY OF TIME**, which says that the past has existed, the present exists, and the future doesn't exist yet. Given this, it could be argued that what exists in time and what exists in eternity are different. In eternity, God is looking out and surveying everything, including the future, even though in time, it does not yet exist.

It could be argued that this criticism is ill-founded. After all, eternity is timelessness, not simply a different kind of time. It might be hard to conceive of how God can know something non-temporally, but the criticism "God cannot know the future now because it does not exist yet" carries little weight, as God does not know the future now, or already. This kind of thinking mistakenly applies temporal concepts to eternity. God knows, according to Boethius, what we would call future as part of the totality of events present to Him in eternity.

Having said this, the idea of events being "present to God in eternity" might raise another problem: what is meant by an eternal present? Boethius and Aquinas's solution to the problem of foreknowledge rests on God being outside of time, but yet they talk about an "eternal present"; how could there be a non-temporal now?

There are two ways to respond to this: The first is to bite the bullet, and say that talking about what God's knowledge is like is difficult because He is non-temporal. We talk about an eternal present because that is our best way of expressing an idea so wholly beyond our experience that no language could capture it.

However, there might be a better solution: one that allows for the idea of something being "present to God in eternity" without relying on temporal language. Imagine a teacher is taking a register:

Teacher: Jimmy?
Jimmy: Present, Miss!

Jimmy is not announcing that he is **NOW**, but he is **HERE**. The word "present" includes, but is not confined to, a temporal meaning. The eternal present could therefore be like Jimmy's presence in the classroom: perhaps everything is present in eternity because it is in some way timelessly there for God to know, rather than because everything is timelessly now for Him.

Still, another criticism remains, that the view of Boethius, and after him Aquinas, strictly does not allow God to foreknow anything, because God knows timelessly; He does not know the future as future. It is hence argued that Boethius and Aquinas are not solving the problem initially raised: they are not finding a way of reconciling God's foreknowledge with our free will.

CONCLUSION

Boethius's solution, developed by Aquinas, is often thought to be the most successful response to the problems with God's foreknowledge, despite the fact that it claims that God has no foreknowledge! As we saw at the beginning of the chapter, we hear in Isaiah that "my thoughts are not your thoughts". Boethius's solution recognises that God's mode of knowing would be different from ours, and accounts for God's otherness whilst retaining His intimate knowledge of His whole creation.

FURTHER READING

CLACK, B & CLACK, BR - The Philosophy of Religion: A Critical Introduction, Polity Press, 2008, Ch. 2 section II

DAVIES, B - An Introduction to The Philosophy of Religion, OUP, 2004, Ch. 9

VARDY, P & ARLISS J - The Thinker's Guide to God, John Hunt Publishing, 2004, Ch. 7

MARENBON, J - Medieval Philosophy: A Historical and Philosophical Introduction, Routledge, 2006, Ch. 5 Study I

Eternity

KEY TERMS

ATEMPORAL - Outside time.

MODIFIED ATEMPORALITY - Not constrained by time, but still relating to time.

SEMPITERNAL - Everlasting.

GOD AND TIME

The question of how God relates to time is one of the most interesting and mysterious of questions concerning God's attributes, because it requires us to think about modes of existing that are utterly different from ours, concerning questions of endless existence or timelessness. God's eternity raises a number of questions: Does God exist in time, as we do, or is He outside of it? Does time exist separately from God, or is it part of God's creation? Is God limited by time, as we are?

There seem to be two possible models of God's relationship with time. On the one hand, there is the possibility that God exists in time, as we do. The other possibility is that God exists outside of time, and that His mode of existence is non-temporal. Both of these visions for God's interaction with time are casually labelled as "God's eternity". In common parlance, "eternal" is a word often used to mean "everlasting", but it can also mean "outside time". We have two quite different models here, and it is therefore important that we properly differentiate them from each other, and find precise vocabulary to express the different views.

GOD IN TIME

Those who say God exists in time claim that the difference between God's and our relationship with time is only one of extent, ie that God has a different duration of existence from us. They claim that God is everlasting, which means that God neither came into nor goes out of existence. He is **SEMPITERNAL**; He exists always. Our life is only of a short span, and God's span of existence is limitless. Still, on this view, God is, like us, part of time, and we can reasonably infer that this model of God would allow for Him also to act in time.

Let's call this **S-ETERNITY**, for sempiternity. S-eternity could be depicted as something like this:

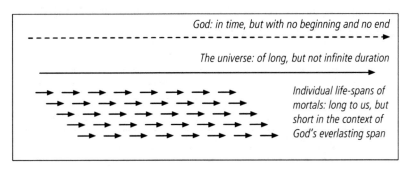

Some would argue that S-eternity is the view that is better represented in the Bible, especially in the Old Testament. Scripture often refers to God as being "everlasting" and His kingdom, laws and words "enduring forever" (we will talk about this in greater detail later). However, the view that God is S-eternal is not that traditionally believed by theologians or philosophers, though there are some modern philosophers, such as **SWINBURNE**, who have taken this view.

GOD OUTSIDE TIME

On the other hand, those who see God as outside of time would claim that God is not simply an everlasting being, but is a being wholly outside the system He created. So on this view, the difference between God's and our relationship with time is much more profound than S-eternity. According to this view, we are temporal, and God is outside of time (**ATEMPORAL**). This means that God's whole mode of existence would be utterly different from our own. On this view, God does not exist in the past, present or future, but timelessly. God's thoughts and actions would have to be timeless, and there are some very interesting questions to be asked about how, or if, this is possible.

Let's call the view that God exists outside time **A-ETERNITY**, for atemporality. A-eternity could be depicted as something like this:

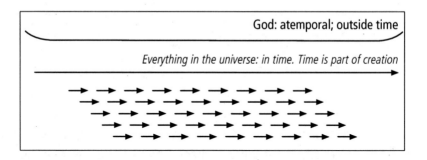

A-eternity is, according to **CLACK AND CLACK**, the traditional view of philosophers and theologians, held by eminent thinkers Augustine, Boethius and Aquinas, though we will see later that Boethius and Aquinas modify the notion as they still wanted God to be able to relate to time. One form of A-eternity or another has, therefore, been a mainstream Christian understanding of God's interaction with time since around the 5th C. Although arguably there is perhaps less biblical support for this view, there are good philosophical reasons supporting it.

So, S-eternity and A-eternity are two possible ways of envisaging how God interacts with time, but which one is the better way of conceiving of God? Well, we need here think about what we mean by "better". Do we mean one that is more philosophically defensible, or do we mean the vision that best reflects what is found in scripture?

TIME AND ETERNITY IN SCRIPTURE

Whenever we examine one of God's supposed attributes, we look both at the impression we get from scripture (the God of Sacred Scripture), as well as what is said in the theological tradition more generally (the God of classical theism). We cannot assume they are necessarily the same.

If we take the Old Testament at face value, it seems that it is portraying an S-eternity view; namely a God that is everlasting, but in time. Evidence for this can be seen both in what the Old Testament explicitly says and what it implies.

In the Psalms, for example, it is explicitly claimed that "before the mountains were born or you brought forth the whole world, from everlasting to everlasting you are God" (Psalm 90:2) and that God sits "enthroned forever; [His] renown endures through all generations". (Psalm 102:12) These, as well as other passages, suggest a God that is S-eternal rather than A-eternal, because they talk of God enduring, not of His being outside of time.

Moreover, if we look at the characteristics God has in the Old Testament, there might be implications for His relationship with time. As parts of the Old Testament have it, God acts in the world; He speaks; He interacts with His creation. These actions must, it seems, take place in time. How could you have a timeless conversation, or a conversation where humans are in time and God is not? The depiction of God in the Old Testament seems to be more consistent with S-eternity than A-eternity.

In the New Testament God is, of course, present in the world in the person of Jesus, and so it seems that Jesus, and by extension God, is in time. However, Christian doctrine claims that Jesus is fully God and fully man, so presumably temporality could be one of his human traits, like eating or having hair. We cannot infer that God is temporal from the fact that Jesus acts in time.

Much of what is said about God's eternity in the New Testament is implied rather than stated, so we have to piece together an impression from what is said. John's Gospel begins with the famous verse:

In the Beginning was The Word
And The Word was with God
And The Word was God.

In a clear echoing of the words of Genesis 1, John seems to be talking about the beginning of time. This idea is deeply problematic in and of itself, because it seems to be talking about a time at which time was created, which is incoherent. Still, even though it is a problematic idea, perhaps it is trying to convey this: that in the beginning of it all, God did not come to be, but God was, just as God always is, being outside of time. Perhaps this is John trying to depict A-eternity.

This view might be corroborated by the seemingly strange thing said by Jesus later on in the Gospel: "Before Abraham was, I am!" The so-called "I am" statements in John are understood by scholars as events where Jesus is proclaiming His divinity. Perhaps here, he is emphasising the A-eternity of God, that what we see as past (the time before Abraham's life) is not just a time when God existed (it does not say "I was"), but is in fact present ("I am") to God.

So, in John there is evidence of the atemporal view. Arguably this continues in the works for Paul, where we hear, for example in Titus 1:2, that Christians have the "hope of eternal life, which God ... promised before the beginning of time". It could be said that this must entail God being outside of time, because He is seen to act before it. Similarly, in 2

Timothy 1:9, we hear that "this grace was given us in Christ Jesus before the beginning of time". Again, it seems that divinity is not constrained by time.

In the Book of Revelation, we hear that God is "the Alpha and the Omega ... who is, and who was, and who is to come, the Almighty." (Rev 1:8) By saying He is the Alpha and Omega (which are the first and last letters of the Greek Alphabet), He is saying that He Himself is the beginning and the end. At first glance, this might look like S-eternity; it is talking about God's existence at the beginning and the end of time. However, it says more than this. It is not just that God exists at the beginning and end, but that God **IS** the beginning and end; He is not governed by time, but governs it.

Many might argue that to try to construct a cogent theory of eternity from the pages of the Bible is futile. For a start, the Bible was written over many centuries by many different people, so it is unlikely to portray one clear idea of how God relates to time. Moreover, trying to capture what it would mean for God to be eternal is difficult, and by saying God endures forever, biblical authors might mean to convey that He is beyond time (more like A-eternity) rather than simply lasting forever (like in S-eternity). We can see from the books of Titus and 2 Timothy how hard it is to convey eternity, because the idea they portray of God acting "before time" clearly makes no sense; how could there be a time before time began? Whatever scripture's concept of God's eternity, attempting to convey **ANY** kind of eternity is problematic. Perhaps, then, we cannot construct an understanding of God's eternity based on what the Bible says.

Summary - time and eternity in scripture

- In the Old Testament, there are many passages that talk of God as everlasting or enduring forever. Also, God is depicted as acting, speaking and interacting with others - all actions that take place in time. Arguably, the Old Testament is portraying an S-eternity view.

- In the New Testament, the nature of God's eternity is spoken of less explicitly, so we have to try to construct an idea of what is being said. There is more evidence in the New Testament of God being beyond time, which might suggest an A-eternity view.

- Much of this needs to be approached cautiously, as it should not be forgotten that scripture is not presented as a worked-through philosophical system. Trying to convey eternity is difficult, so we cannot be sure of any conclusions we draw based on what is said; we need to allow for poetic licence.

GOD'S ETERNITY IN THE TRADITION OF CLASSICAL THEISM

As we said in the introduction, the purpose of the philosophical/ theological work undertaken by thinkers in the tradition of classical theism - Augustine, Boethius and Aquinas - was not to deny the scriptural tradition, but to interpret it and create a coherent philosophical system around it. In this philosophical tradition, A-eternity is the best represented view, even though that does not always mean a God utterly separate from time; the God of classical theism is not a God that simply exists forever.

Augustine

In Book XI of his **CONFESSIONS**, Augustine's aims for a theory of eternity are made very clear: he is looking for an idea of eternity that is "true eternity". Augustine is arguing for an atemporal God. He tells us that it is hard to conceive of eternity, because time passes, and eternity stands still. He is not thinking of eternity as simply "forever" or "infinite time", but rather "outside time". Augustine argues that time began with God's creation of the universe. God did not sit around twiddling His thumbs until He felt like creating a universe. God exists in "an ever-present eternity", (Book XI, Ch. xiii) not in time. Time is part of God's creation.

Boethius

In Book V, Ch. vi of his **CONSOLATION OF PHILOSOPHY**, Boethius defines eternity as "the possession of endless life whole and perfect at a single moment". As with Augustine, we see the idea of eternity as separate from the passing of time. Eternity is a moment, but not one that passes, rather one that is "whole and perfect". If God's eternity meant only that He always existed, (S-eternity), then moments would come and go for God, just as they do for us. Boethius claims that "that which includes and possesses the whole fullness of unending life at once, from which nothing future is absent, from which nothing past has escaped, this is rightly called eternal". In other words, eternity must include a grasp on all time at once, indeed as one. This reflects both the "ever-present" notion of eternity that we see in Augustine's work, but also adds a notion that time is a deficient version of eternity; that God's existence has a wholeness and fullness unattainable in time. This is not a vision of atemporality that depicts a God utterly devoid of an understanding of time but rather one of being both outside time as well as having a grasp of it.

Aquinas

Aquinas's views on time and eternity were influenced heavily by Augustine and Boethius, as well as Aristotle. One could argue that much of what Aquinas says about time and eternity takes and builds on Boethius's and Augustine's work. Nevertheless, this is not to say that Aquinas does this uncritically: it was part of his method to include objections to the authorities he was using.

Aquinas's view, like those of Augustine and Boethius before him, is not one of S-eternity; God does not just exist at all times but is outside the limitations of the temporal sphere. However **JOHN MARENBON** argues that, as with Boethius, we cannot unreservedly say that Aquinas thought God was completely outside of time either, because Aquinas seems to think of "God's eternity as embracing all things in time". (An Introduction to Medieval Philosophy by John Marenbon, p. 254) Atemporality means outside time, but Aquinas's view of eternity is one that allows for God to be both outside time and yet to encompass it. Both Aquinas and Boethius's views might best be described as "modified A-eternity".

Modified A-eternity could be depicted as follows:

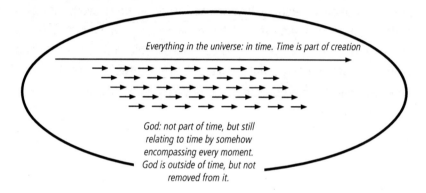

Everything in the universe: in time. Time is part of creation

God: not part of time, but still relating to time by somehow encompassing every moment. God is outside of time, but not removed from it.

REASONS TO THINK GOD MUST BE A-ETERNAL

There are good philosophical and theological reasons to think that God must be outside of time. As Genesis and the Gospel of John both tell us, "In the beginning" God existed. If we agree with Augustine's reading of the creation in Genesis, it makes sense to say that time began at the creation, because otherwise we have a picture of God idly waiting around in time until He could be bothered to create the world; hardly the actions of a loving God, and a rather strangely anthropomorphic depiction of the Almighty.

Moreover, if God exists in time, we are faced with difficulties for God's omnipotence. The first difficulty seems to be that if God exists in time, He did not create it, and presumably He does not control it. Indeed, this would mean that there was something that is very much part of the universe, but yet for which God would not be responsible. If God did not create time, then its existence is not adequately explained by God in the way that His creation might be; where did time come from?

Further, if God does not control time, indeed cannot control time, then does He not become a little too much like us, rather than something beyond human characteristics and experience? This does not seem like a vision of an omnipotent God. A God existing in time, with no control over it, seems more like Zeus or Thor than the God of Christianity.

Second, the idea of God being in time seems to conflict with the idea of God as immutable (unchanging). If God is in time, then it is true to say that in the past, God was, in the present, God is, and God will be in the future but that means that He, in some way, is bound to change.

This example should make the problem clear:

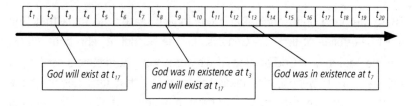

If we take the various boxes labelled t_1, t_2 and so on to represent different moments in time, and the arrow to represent God's sempiternal existence, we can see that different things will end up being true about God at different times. At t_2, it is true to say that God will exist at t_{17}, but to make the same claim at t_{22} would be false. Similarly, the statement "God was in existence at t_3 and will exist at t_{17}" is true between t_4 and t_{16}, and at no other time. If a statement about God can be true at one time and false at another, the true things we can say about God change, and so we might infer that His immutability has been compromised.

This problem is compounded if you consider that God acts in time. Say God creates the world at t_1. This means that at t_1, He is doing something, and then, perhaps at t_2, He is resting, or doing something else. This is not a picture of an unchanging God. It seems that a sempiternal God cannot also be an immutable God.

These problems do not arise for an atemporal God. If God is not part of time, then it is not true to say "God was in existence at t_3 and will exist at t_{17}", but rather just "God exists" or "God is"; these will always be true of God on the atemporal view.

REASONS TO THINK GOD MUST BE S-ETERNAL

There are, however, problems with God being atemporal. If God is outside time, it seems difficult to account for how it could be that God acts. If God is timeless, how could He create, or speak, or send a plague, or give commandments? These events do not occur timelessly, but rather occur at specific times and for specific durations. A God that is in time can act in time - no problem there (except for His immutability) - but the idea of an atemporal God that acts in time is troublesome.

It could be argued that those who advocate an immutable, timeless God are defending a **DEIST** idea of God; one where God is at one remove from the world. This is at odds with the idea of a God who is involved in the world and cares about it. A sempiternal God might seem less powerful than one who is not constrained by time, but at least it is an idea that allows for God to have a relationship with His creation. If God is outside time, He is arguably too far away from theism to be the God of Christianity.

ETERNAL ACTS

Aquinas's modified A-eternity seeks to overcome this dilemma, offering a God who is not carried along by time's flow, but can still relate to time, and is not entirely abstracted from His creation. Aquinas said that God, as a wholly simple being (one that is one substance and indivisible into parts), means that His actions are the same as His being. So, God's actions must be the same as His Nature. As an eternal being, they must be non-temporal. Aquinas formulated the idea of God's single, timeless act that on earth, through the prism of time would be felt as different events.

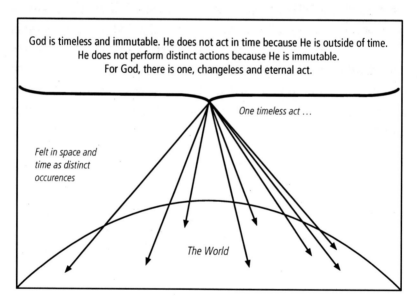

God is timeless and immutable. He does not act in time because He is outside of time. He does not perform distinct actions because He is immutable. For God, there is one, changeless and eternal act.

One timeless act ...

Felt in space and time as distinct occurences

The World

CONCLUSION

Perhaps the solution offered by Aquinas gives us everything we need from a theory of God's eternity. It does not make God subject to time in the way He must surely be if he is S-eternal, but it avoids the difficulty of God seeming removed from His creation that a strict A-eternity view gives us. It is, perhaps then the modified A-eternity of Boethius and Aquinas that gives us what we need from a theory of God's eternity.

FURTHER READING

CLACK, B & CLACK, BR - The Philosophy of Religion: A Critical Introduction, Polity Press, 2008, Ch. 2 section II

DAVIES, B - An Introduction to The Philosophy of Religion, OUP, 2004, Ch. 9

VARDY, P & ARLISS J - The Thinker's Guide to God, John Hunt Publishing, 2004, Ch. 7

MARENBON, J - Medieval Philosophy: A Historical and Philosophical Introduction, Routledge, 2006, Ch. 5 Study I

Postscript

Clare Jarmy read Philosophy at St Catharine's College Cambridge, before training to be a teacher. She is Head of Philosophy and Religious Studies at Bedales School in Hampshire.

Students seeking fuller explanations and a bibliography should also consult the website which also contains exam tips and past questions listed by theme.